THE MAKING OF A
Queen

THE MAKING OF A
Queen

Linda Doeser

GALLERY BOOKS

Published in The United States by
GALLERY BOOKS
An imprint of W.H. Smith Publishers Inc., 112 Madison Avenue, New
York, 10016

ISBN 0 8317 5701-9

Printed in Italy

Camera Press: 38, 55 bottom, 57 bottom, 59, 60, 62 right, 82 top right, 83, 102; Mike Anthony 24, 112; Ken Goff 50, 96/7; Glenn Harvey, Back cover bottom left, 87, 93; N Hinkes 61 top, 65 bottom left, 55 top; Graham Horton 73; JS Library 8 bottom, 57 centre left, 65 top; Pat Lyttle 62 centre; Bernard Morton 61 bottom, 64 bottom left, 65 bottom right, 88; Richard Open 95; Terry Spencer 15; Mark Stewart 82 bottom, 89.

Hulton Picture Company: Back cover top and bottom right, 2, 7, 8 top, 9 bottom, 9 top, 10, 11, 12, 14, 16, 17, 19, 20, 21, 23, 25, 26, 28, 29, 31, 32, 33, 35, 36, 37, 39, 41 bottom, 41 top, 42, 43, 44 bottom, 44 top, 4/5, 45 bottom, 45 top, 47, 49, 51, 53, 57 centre right, 57 top, 62 left, 64 bottomright, 64 top, 68, 69, 71, 72, 74, 75, 76, 77, 78, 79, 80, 82 top left, 83 top, 84, 85, 86, 91, 92, 97, 99, 101, 108, 109, 26/7, 104/5, 106/7, 110/1.

JS Library: Front cover.

CONTENTS

CHAPTER 1
NO
CINDERELLA

One of the most popular and endearing of all fairytales is that of Cinderella, the story of a poor but beautiful scullerymaid rescued from a life of drudgery by a handsome prince and taken off to a world of luxury, all with the aid of a fairy godmother.

Journalists seem to find the Cinderella story irresistible when it comes to writing about the courtship and marriage of Charles and Diana. Even the most experienced professional finds her sophisticated heart melting. For example, the usually cool Suzanne Lowry, once Woman's Editor of the *Guardian* wrote, 'A luminous, wraith-like beauty, giving her an aura of Cinderella' – and this is one of the less extravagant effusions. They should all know better because the story of Charles and Diana is about as far from that of Cinderella as it could be.

First, Lady Diana Spencer was certainly not poor. On the contrary, she was born into one of the wealthiest and most aristocratic families in Britain. When she moved to London in 1977, she went straight into a £100,000 flat owned by her father, and was shortly afterwards given a car. It is doubtful whether Diana had any experience of sculleries, and although her life and work in London probably had their dull moments, they could scarcely be described as drudgery. Equally, rather than Highgrove, her first home with Prince Charles, providing a new life of unaccustomed luxury, it is actually smaller and less luxurious than her own family's country house at Althorp in Northamptonshire.

But there were some real-life parallels with the fairytale. Diana was beautiful, her prince was handsome and there was no shortage of 'fairy godmothers' among

Previous page: Lady Diana Spencer was plagued by press and by rumour as soon as her association with Prince Charles became public knowledge. She behaved with grace and good manners throughout her ordeal. Here, she is seen leaving the kindergarten in St George's Square in London, where she worked.

Above: When she first went to live in London, Diana shared a flat with friends in Coleherne Court.

Left: No Cinderella – but the shy young Diana blossomed into womanhood and beauty when she was married. She is shown here dancing with her Prince.

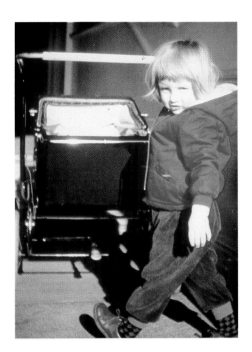

Above: An early photo-call – a very young Diana eyes the camera with some suspicion.

her family, her friends and even the Royal Family, all dedicated to supporting the romance towards its great climax at St Paul's.

With the benefit of hindsight, it is now obvious that Diana was the ideal Princess of Wales, but to begin with, she was not even in the field, let alone among the identified runners. She was born on 1 July, 1961 at Park House on the Sandringham estate in Norfolk in the same room as her mother had been born 25 years earlier. Park House is a comfortable mansion which the Spencers rented from the Royal Family their nearby neighbours at Sandringham House. Park House had been particularly useful for Diana's grandfather, Lord Fermoy, when he was Conservative Member of Parliament for King's Lynn, the local market town. It had another advantage: a large, heated swimming pool which was very popular with the Windsor children when the Queen was in residence.

Diana had a normal childhood for a girl from her background. She had a nanny and then a governess, Gertrude Allen, who had also been her mother's governess. Miss Allen remembers her younger charge as a happy child. Naturally, Diana was used to the attention of servants from an early age.

She was an active little girl with two older sisters who behaved as all older sisters do – with love, protection, and a fair measure of affectionate bullying. Another person who grew to know Diana well was the gracious and friendly lady from the adjacent house who became sufficiently familiar to be addressed as 'Aunt Lillibet'. So Diana's early years already distinguished her lifestyle from that of many people who will one day be her husband's subjects.

Right: An attractive child with blonde hair and blue eyes, Diana looks up shyly through her lashes with an expression that was to become familiar throughout Britain some 16 years later.

THE SPENCER FAMILY

The Spencer family has a long connection with the Royal Family, and both the Prince and Princess of Wales share a common ancestor in James I. Interestingly, Lady Diana was the first Englishwoman in more than 300 years to marry the heir to the throne. The last occasion was when her ancestor, Lady Anne Hyde, married the future James II.

The Spencers are indeed a special family and can trace their direct lineage to an ancestor who was Lord Chief Justice to Edward II in the 14th century. However, apart from this distinguished lawyer, the family's fortune and distinction has come from commerce rather than law. The Spencers were successful sheep farmers in the Middle Ages when English wool was a valuable commodity. They amassed a great fortune from the wool trade and, in the late 15th century, John Spencer financed the acquisition of a large tract of land in Northamptonshire from the Abbot of Evesham. This was to become Althorp, although, at the time, there was only a comparatively small medieval building on the site. The family continued to make their main home at Wormleighton, a Warwickshire estate where they already owned a large mansion. The sale took a long time to complete and it was 1506 before Althorp was finally Spencer land. Two years later John Spencer built himself a sizeable red-brick mansion and surrounded it with a moat. This forms the core of Althorp as it is today although there were many later modifications and additions.

John, the first Earl Spencer, was a descendant of the junior branch of the family, the senior branch becoming the Dukes of Marlborough.

Successive generations of Spencers continued to increase their fortune and, with it, their power and patronage. Henry VIII bestowed a knighthood on John Spencer. By the time of Elizabeth I, the Spencers were considered to be one of the richest families in England. Monarchs were always in need of money and the support and friendship of powerful families. It was no surprise, therefore, that in 1603 James I made plain Sir Robert Spencer into Baron Spencer of Wormleighton, which was still the family's main home. Not that the mansion at Althorp was in any sense unworthy. In fact, the new baron entertained the Queen of Denmark there and commissioned Ben Jonson to write a new masque specially for the occasion.

Robert's son married Lady Penelope Wriothsley and they also used Althorp for royal entertainment. In 1634 a great banquet was served to Charles I and Queen Henrietta Maria. It was so expensive that the family has kept the bills to this day.

The third baron, Henry, married another beautiful heiress, Lady Dorothy Sidney, whose grace and charm are enshrined as 'Sacharissa' in the poem of Edmund Weller. The famous poem 'Go, lovely rose...' is dedicated to her. Diana, as one might guess, has some great beauties in her pedigree. Henry was a very young man when he married his lovely wife and she quickly presented him with four children. At the beginning of the English Civil War, Henry joined the royalist army and lent Charles I, who was always short of money, £10,000, an enormous sum of money at the time. In return, the King granted him the title Earl of Sunderland, but he was not to enjoy his new status for long. Only four

Viscount Althorp, Diana's younger brother and heir to the earldom, conducts parties of visitors around the family home, which is now open to the public.

months later, the 23-year-old Earl was killed at the Battle of Newbury. Not long afterwards, Prince Rupert burned down the mansion at Wormleighton to prevent his Roundhead enemies turning it into a fortress. The young widow and her family were forced to move permanently to Althorp, where the Spencer family has been ever since.

Young Henry's eldest son, Robert, succeeded to the title at the age of two and grew up to be an astute politician. Charles II returned from exile in 1660 and soon showed favour to the wealthy young Earl, appointing him Secretary of State. Robert Spencer was later a trusted adviser to James II and then to his successor William III.

But it was not the second Earl's political success that most benefited the Spencer family. An ambitious man, he felt that the grounds in which Althorp stood were too provincial for someone of his standing. So he commissioned Andre le Nôtre, who had designed the extraordinary gardens of Versailles, to give Althorp a new setting. Le Nôtre set to work with a will and soon Althorp was at the centre of a number of magnificent pathways and grand avenues. The second Earl also filled the house with paintings he had bought during his long years abroad in the service of the Royal Family. His wife, Lady Anne Digby, inherited even more splendid works of art from her mother, and together these form the basis of the world-famous collection at Althorp today.

John Evelyn, the Restoration diarist, wrote of Althorp :

The house or rather palace at Althorp is a noble uniform pile in form of a half H built of brick and freestone balustered and à la moderne; the hall is well, the staircase excellent; the rooms of state galleries, office and furniture such as may become a great prince.

The richness of Althorp has certainly not diminished in the years since. Early in the 18th century, Charles, third Earl of Sunderland and Prime Minister in the reign of George I, married the daughter of the first Duke of Marlborough. Later the fifth Earl of Sunderland became the third Duke of Marlborough, and his younger brother succeeded to Althorp. Thus the Spencer family was divided into two: the senior branch becoming the Dukes of Marlborough and the junior being the Spencers. The first Earl Spencer was created in 1705 and married yet another noted beauty. The family's fine features were captured by both Gainsborough and Reynolds, adding even more great paintings to the Althorp collection.

George, the second Earl had a distinguished political career, being successively Lord Privy Seal, First Lord of the Admiralty, Ambassador to Vienna, and finally Home Secretary. He also married a famous beauty, Lavinia Bingham. George III and Queen Charlotte were godparents to their daughter. Close relationships and friendships with Kings and Queens echo throughout the Spencer family history, and Diana was by no means the first Spencer to be on first name terms with the Royal Family.

The next and third Earl Spencer was also an active and successful politician. He was Leader of the House of Commons during the Grey administration, and in the 1830s was Chancellor of the Exchequer. He turned down the office of Prime Minister, saying that he preferred farming. Indeed he helped found the Royal Agricultural College at Cirencester where, much later, Captain Mark Phillips, husband of the Princess Royal, was to be a student. His wife died giving birth to a stillborn child so the title eventually passed to his brother Frederick. A professional sailor with the rank of Rear-Admiral, he was later appointed Lord Chamberlain.

Frederick's son, John, maintained a family tradition by becoming First Lord

Althorp boasts a magnificent collection of Old Masters and other works of art collected over many centuries. The present Earl is seen here on the grand staircase sharing his knowledge of family history with his son, Charles.

The Spencer family has a long and distinguished history of service to the crown and to the state, being both loyal servants and good friends to a succession of monarchs. The fifth Earl, shown here in traditional regalia, was First Lord of the Admiralty, Keeper of the Privy Seal and Lord Lieutenant of Ireland.

of the Admiralty from 1892-95, Keeper of the Privy Seal and, twice, Lord Lieutenant of Ireland when this was anything but a sinecure. His beautiful wife was known in Dublin society as 'Spencer's Fairy Queen'.

The last earl of the Victorian era was succeeded by his half-brother, who became successively Lord Chamberlain to both Edward VII and George V. His eldest son succeeded in 1922.

The Spencer family includes, in descent from Charles II and the Duchess of Cleveland, two Dukes of Grafton, a Marchioness of Hertford, and an admiral. The line of descent from Sir Winston Churchill, father of the first Duke of Marlborough, includes the fourth Duke of Bedford and the first Duke of Devonshire. From the line of Charles II and Lucy Walters are four Earls of Lucan, and from the King and the Duchess of Portsmouth, five Dukes of Richmond, the sixth Duke of Bedford, and four Dukes of Abercorn.

DIANA'S FAMILY CIRCLE

Lady Diana's father, the present Earl, was born in 1924, and educated at Eton and the Royal Military Academy at Sandhurst. He later took a course at the Royal Agricultural College at Cirencester. As Viscount Althorp (the title of the current Earl's eldest son), he served with the Royal Scots Greys in World War II, becoming ADC to the Governor of South Australia in 1947, and Equerry to George VI in 1950. During this time in his life he was often a guest at Balmoral where he joined shooting parties which also included Prince Philip. In 1928 when George VI was still the Duke of York, he had hunted with the Pytchley Hunt at Althorp.

Diana's father is the eighth Earl Spencer. He inherited the title from his grandfather when Diana was 14 years old, and the family moved from Park House on the Sandringham Estate to the grand and imposing Althorp House. He continued the Spencer tradition of royal service and was Equerry to both King George VI and to Queen Elizabeth.

15

When George VI died in 1952, Earl Spencer became Equerry to Queen Elizabeth II. He accompanied Her Majesty and the Duke of Edinburgh on their Commonwealth Tour of 1953-54. When he was acting Master of the Royal Household, he married the Honourable Frances Roche, daughter of Lord and Lady Fermoy at Westminster Abbey on 1 June, 1954. The Queen, the Queen Mother, Princess Margaret and Princess Alexandra were guests at the service, one of the Society events of the year. Lady Frances Spencer was the youngest bride to be married at Westminster Abbey for 50 years.

Five children were born: three daughters and two sons, one of whom, John, died in the year of his birth in 1960. Their second son, Charles, Viscount Althorp, was born in 1964, the same year as Prince Edward.

Lady Sarah Spencer was born in 1955, and the Queen was godmother at her christening. After she left school she began working in London on the staff of *Vogue* magazine. During this time her name came to be linked with that of Prince Charles when they were frequently seen together at polo matches, Royal Ascot and at Sandringham, where Lady Sarah was a guest of the Queen. She was one of the Prince of Wales's skiing party at Klosters, and this escalated newspaper conjecture that the two would marry, but, in the true sense of the words, they were, and are, 'just good friends'. Lady Sarah married Neil McCorquodale in 1980. Lady Sarah Armstrong-Jones, daughter of Princess Margaret, was a bridesmaid.

Lady Jane Spencer was born in 1957. The Queen Mother was one of her godparents, and the Duke of Kent another. Lady Jane was one of the bridesmaids at the Duke's wedding to Miss Katharine Worsley at York Minster in 1961. None of the Spencer girls were debutantes, and, like her elder sister, Lady Jane also worked on the staff of *Vogue* magazine. In 1978, she married Sir Richard Fellowes, Assistant Secretary to the Queen, at the Guards' Chapel in London.

Diana's parents, the then Viscount Althorp and the Hon. Frances Roche, were married at Westminster Abbey in June 1954. At 18 years old, she was the youngest bride to be married in the Abbey for 50 years. Royal guests at the wedding included the Queen and the Duke of Edinburgh.

16

EARLY YEARS

Throughout her childhood and teens Lady Diana Frances Spencer would have been aware of her family's close connections with royalty, both from the pictures on the walls at Althorp and from splashing about in the heated pool with the Windsor boys.

Once she had outgrown her governess, Diana's education followed conventional lines. She went to a nursery school in King's Lynn and then to a preparatory school at Diss, a market town also in Norfolk. She was, as her headmistress records, 'a perfectly ordinary little girl who is always kind and cheerful'. She was fond of pets, preferring small creatures such as gerbils, hamsters and guinea pigs.

When Diana was six years old her parents divorced after a long period during which their marriage had deteriorated beyond redemption. It was an acrimonious affair played against a background of unpleasant publicity in the tabloids. Diana's father was given custody of the children. Diana's mother married Peter Shand-Kydd, heir to a wallpaper fortune, and moved to his estate in North West Scotland. Her ordeal by tabloid and papparazzi was to prove a useful experience a dozen years later when she helped her daughter endure the intrusive attentions of the press.

In the same way as her sisters Diana progressed from prep school to boarding school. At the age of 12 she went to West Heath, near Sevenoaks in Kent.

Diana as a pre-teenager showed early signs of her future good looks. Later, her chic and fashion sense were to become a byword, so this grown-up and stylish hat is an interesting feature.

Coincidentally, the last Princess of Wales, later Queen Mary, had been one of its pupils. Diana enjoyed music and dancing rather than academic lessons, although she was interested in history. She wanted to become a ballet dancer, but grew too tall. (She still keeps up her dancing practice to keep fit.) At West Heath, Diana was taught alongside girls of the same social class; girls she would meet later, with different names and titles, throughout the rest of her life. She made friends of whom her parents approved and with whom they would allow her to share a flat when she eventually moved to London. The Princess of Wales remains good friends with two 'old girls', Carolyn Pride and Anne Beckwith-Smith, the latter now one of her Ladies-in-Waiting. While she was at West Heath she maintained her friendship with the Royal Family, exchanging letters with Prince Andrew who is only two years older than her. In fact, this friendship provoked some thoughtful speculation among family and friends. For some, she was never less than a potential royal partner.

After her parents' divorce, Diana continued to live at Park House but spent frequent holidays with her mother in Scotland. When she was 14, her grandfather, the seventh Earl, died and her father succeeded to the title. The family moved to Althorp, and Park House, the scene of so many happy and youthful meetings with the royal children, has stood empty to this day.

Althorp must have seemed a vast and even forbidding place to live after the more domestic comforts of Park House. There is some evidence, too, that Earl Spencer, never a very communicative man, had led a rather lonely life after the divorce. This may have been accentuated at Althorp with the responsibilities of running a large house and estate. With her mother hundreds of miles away, it must have sometimes been difficult for the girl who was one day to become Princess of Wales.

But suddenly, everything changed. Within a year of his arrival at Althorp John Spencer met and fell in love with the Countess of Dartmouth, better known as Raine, daughter of the famous romantic novelist Barbara Cartland. In less than a year, they were married and Althorp had a Countess in residence.

At first, the Spencer children did not know how to take this colourful addition to the family circle. Children, especially teenagers, are notoriously conservative and even intolerant in such matters. At the age of 15, always a difficult age for girls, Diana must have been more than a little disturbed. In fact, the new Countess proved to be a necessary and vigorous new broom. She organized her husband's affairs so that the heavy death duties encumbering his estate were settled, superfluous staff paid or pensioned off and a profitable shop opened in the stables for the coachloads of visitors who were now encouraged to visit Althorp.

Diana continued to see her mother regularly and spent many happy times on the Shand-Kydd estate. There was, and remains, much affection between mother and daughter.

Raine's arrival had a more significant effect on the fortunes of the Spencer family. Three years after his marriage and just after a party thrown to celebrate the estate's debts finally being paid off, Diana's father suddenly suffered a massive stroke. He was so near to death that a lesser woman would have given up, but Raine Spencer threw all her formidable resources of energy into saving her husband's life. He had had a severe haemorrhage followed by double pneumonia. It says a lot for the Earl's constitution as well as his wife's determination that he made a full recovery and soon returned to his duties as master of Althorp. It was a harrowing time for Diana.

Opposite: Diana likes to keep in touch with her girlhood friends. She is seen here at the wedding of her ex-schoolfriend and ex-flatmate, Carolyn Pride, at Chelsea Old Church in 1982. She was also a guest at Anne Bolton's wedding and made a special point of visiting her old friend during her trip to Australia.

During her last term at West Heath, Lady Diana went home to Althorp and Lady Sarah re-introduced her 16-year-old sister to the Prince of Wales 'in a field', as she herself later put it. Prince Charles was one of the guests invited to a shooting party on the estate.

On reaching 16 and leaving West Heath, Lady Diana went to a finishing school in Switzerland, the Institut Alpin near Videmanette near Gstaad. Here she improved her French and, among other things, her skiing, cooking and domestic science. However, for some reason or other, Diana could not stand the place and after only six weeks she packed her bags and left for home. Homesickness and concern for her father's health are the obvious reasons for this abrupt departure; of course some journalists have made every effort to find a juicy scandal which would make a 'good' story. Nothing has been found. But the event does indicate a strong will and an independence of spirit, a refusal to be cowed by a staff who must have been accustomed to dealing with recalcitrant young women.

Diana returned home when her father was still recovering from his stroke and, understandably, the focus of attention at Althorp was on him and his wife's valiant efforts on his behalf. There was little or no opportunity to show any useful filial devotion. In short, she was better off out of the way. The obvious place to go was London, where she had plenty of friends and there was always something to do. The Spencers owned property there, including a flat at Coleherne Court in South Kensington where Diana could live safely and sensibly. Arrangements were quickly made and three trustworthy and reliable friends moved in to share the flat with her. These included Carolyn Pride, who was, at that time, studying music. Like many girls of her age, Diana enjoyed shopping in fashionable Knightsbridge, running a household and meeting her friends. Many would say she was a typical 'Sloane Ranger', a term used to describe the young people living in and around Chelsea and Sloane Square in London and who established a style all their own. They were to be seen at all the right places, and were always 'noticed' when they went to the Badminton Horse Trials, for instance, sporting the inevitable 'wellies' and invariably accompanied by the ever-popular Jack Russell terrier.

Diana took a course in Cordon Bleu cooking and, almost by accident, also found herself looking after a two-year old American boy called Patrick, taking him out for walks and generally amusing him. This soon led her to take a job with the Young England Kindergarten in Pimlico run by her friends Victoria Wilson and Kay Seth Smith, both former pupils of West Heath. In doing this, she discovered an occupation she was good at and really enjoyed. She taught her young charges drawing, painting, and nursery songs and all the other things small children do at kindergarten.

Alongside working at the kindergarten Diana continued to lead a busy social life. She passed her driving test at the age of 17, she visited friends and relatives, she took holidays both at Althorp and with her mother in Scotland. She went skiing in Switzerland. In fact, while she was in Switzerland during her short stay at finishing school, she had accepted an invitation to a skiing holiday at Klosters hosted by Prince Charles. It was a totally unremarked upon but momentous occasion. Although ostensibly he was with his accepted girl friend Lady Sarah Spencer, it was the first time he had had a good look at her younger sister. With the gift of hindsight, we now know that this was the very first step towards the making of a queen.

CHAPTER 2
THE
ROMANCE

In about a dozen years' time, the tabloids will begin to feature pictures of Prince William in the company of pretty girls and there will be rumours of a royal romance. However much he and his parents may contradict, protest, or deny, the world's media will show an insatiable appetite for stories about a future Princess of Wales. Many a hapless young woman will find herself suddenly harried by reporters and photographers because she has been seen twice with the handsome young prince. William, of course, will long have been immune to this ordeal by media through a lifetime of over-exposure to photographers and reporters – and certainly entirely cynical about the constant distortions, fabrications and straight lies about himself and his love-life.

One day, by the nature of things, the Prince will meet the woman he will eventually want to marry and there will begin a long crescendo of media obsession with her, her family, her friends and every tiny detail of her life. At this point, Charles and Diana will no doubt exchange rueful smiles. This has all happened before – to them. It reflects the deep and abiding interest of millions of ordinary people in what has to be an extraordinary romance. And this interest, in turn, reflects the true importance – dynastic and constitutional – of the marriage of a future king and queen.

Previous page: Charles and Diana managed to snatch only a few private moments together once their love affair became public. Balmoral provided the ideal quiet setting for the young lovers.

Below: When Prince William grows up, he will probably endure the rumours about his future bride with fortitude. But, somewhere, even now, is the little girl who will one day be his Princess and later his Queen. She will certainly be very grateful for the advice and guidance of her future mother-in-law who knows all the problems first-hand.

ENSURING THE SUCCESSION

The need to secure the succession has obsessed nearly all monarchs and their advisers for centuries. Henry VIII desperately needed a male heir and went to horrific and bloody lengths to sire one. His daughter Elizabeth drove her advisers almost crazy with her refusal to marry. Even today, when the line of succession has been worked out to the remotest possible degree, any unexpected hitch would cause a great deal of public unease.

More recently in history we know that Victoria and Albert had many earnest discussions about their son Edward's future bride, and Victoria called on the services of many advisers, including her married daughter Vicky and her admired and trusted chief courtier Baron Stockmar, to help her find a suitable candidate. Their hunt through the royal courts of Europe and their less-than-flattering comments about the various royal and noble ladies they scrutinized make for entertaining reading today, but it was all deadly serious at the time.

Princess Marie of Altenburg dressed badly and had 'a most disagreeable mother'. Stockmar thought Princess Elizabeth of Weid 'dowdy', but Vicky

From birth, Prince Charles was destined to be King. He has been raised and trained with this future duty always in mind and with the example of his mother before him. For his future Queen, no such years of training were possible.

disagreed with him and said she had 'a very fresh complexion and nice white teeth, a great many freckles and a mark of a leaf on one cheek that does not show much'. She also 'had not a pretty nose and rather a long chin'. She also had a tendency to use bad language, which would hardly have endeared her to the strait-laced Queen Victoria.

Princess Anna of Hesse had 'an incipient twitching in her eyes and an abrupt way of speaking'. Princess Marie of Hohenzollern-Sigmaringen was 'quite lovely', but a non-starter because she was a Catholic. (You may remember the British media's brief but avid flirtation in the 1970s with the idea of Princess Marie Astrid of Luxembourg as a possible bride for Prince Charles.) The Princess of Sweden was too young, while the Princess of Desan was too old.

Eventually, attention began to focus on Princess Alexandra of Denmark. It is fair to say that the exertions of Princess Vicky and Baron Stockmar proved to be remarkably successful. Alexandra of Denmark was indeed the ideal future consort for the youthful Prince. She passed Queen Victoria's stern scrutiny as a suitable Princess of Wales and, in time, her successor as Queen.

It was often said that Queen Alexandra liked lapdogs and knick-knacks while her husband liked ladies! But she was very tolerant of his friendships, and their marriage was a happy one. She took a keen interest in charity and was especially interested in nursing, showing sympathy and understanding with the cause and status of the profession. She instituted Alexandra Rose Day, a charity devoted to medical needs. In World War I, she was Patron of the Silver Thimble Fund for war charities and often visited wounded soldiers in hospitals. In 1916 she autographed programmes for an entertainment given by the King and Queen for the wounded. Very sensitive and sympathetic, she even wrote special personal messages on wreaths for funerals, and attended the memorial service for Edith Cavell in 1919.

An especial interest was the welfare of children. A special feast for poor children was held to celebrate Queen Victoria's Jubilee, for which the Princess of Wales made the ice cream. A children's review was held in Hyde Park in London with more than 10,000 children attending. A beautiful, tolerant and much loved Queen, she died in 1925.

When the time came to choose a bride for Eddie, the eldest son of the Prince and Princess of Wales, Queen Victoria was still on the throne and once more insisted on playing a very active role in the selection procedure. By now, her descendents occupied many of the thrones of Europe and so she had a unique and unprecedented knowledge of the royal runners. But there were problems. Eddie, born in 1864 and heir to the Prince of Wales, had turned out to be dull witted and dissipated – a sad disappointment to his parents. Nevertheless, he would necessarily become Prince of Wales and in due course King, so a bride had to be found.

Luckily, there was one at hand in the person of Victoria Mary, Duchess of Teck, the daughter of a German duke and grand-daughter of King George III. Although she was officially German, she had been born in Kensington Palace and had spent the whole of her life in Britain. Queen Victoria did not care much for her mother, but she had cast a favourable eye on the serious young Princess and had early marked her out as a possible wife for her grandson Eddie. Their engagement was announced in December 1891. Within a month the Prince caught pneumonia and died at the age of 27. His younger brother George was a much more suitable heir to the throne, with no obvious character defects and a strong sense of duty. If Princess Mary, or May as she was often known, would

Above: Like all brides, Diana had to find her place within her new family, but for her the task was harder because this adjustment had to be made in the public spotlight. Her spontaneously warm personality and innate sensitivity have enabled her to strike a very successful balance.

Left: The Prince of Wales' coat of arms with its motto 'ICH DIEN'.

have made a good Queen for Eddie, she would make an even better one for George. With the Queen's encouragement and approval, their engagement was announced, and they were duly married the next year.

Arranged marriages like this can hardly be described as a love-match, but, in fact, this one turned out to be a remarkably successful partnership. He had reluctantly abandoned his chosen career as a professional sailor and she provided unyielding support as Queen Consort throughout his reign.

A tall, commanding figure, Queen Mary earned the love and respect of all for her courage and fortitude in the face of much adversity. She suffered the death of three of her sons, but bore it stoically. She loved shopping and collecting antiques. During World War II, when resident in Gloucestershire, she often visited Bristol and Bath after bombing raids, and paused to look at the shops as well. She also visited many hospitals and factories in the area. She gave orders that any servicemen seen walking were to be given lifts in her car – much to their delight and surprise! Queen Mary was a lady of the old order – every inch a Queen in manner and looks, earning love and respect everywhere.

Their eldest son, Edward, was born during the lifetime of Queen Victoria, who attended his christening: there is a famous four-generation photograph of the old Queen sitting and cradling him, while her son and grandson stand by. Edward turned out to be a highly successful Prince of Wales in his earlier days – handsome, dashing and sociable. He was a great favourite with the British people, who were very impressed with his daredevil feats on the hunting field and race track. His romance and marriage to the twice-divorced Wallis Simpson rocked the country and fascinated the world. Unable, as he said himself, to reign without the woman he loved at his side, he abdicated in December 1936.

Edward VIII's younger brother, George, Duke of York became King. He had never expected this sudden and unwelcome elevation. King George VI was a gentle and kindly man, thrust into the limelight by the abdication of his elder brother, and would have preferred to live quietly. He was undoubtedly helped and sustained throughout his reign by his Queen. Born the Lady Elizabeth Bowes-Lyon, she was the youngest but one of a family of 10 children of the Earl and Countess of Strathmore, whose Scottish home was the historic Glamis Castle. Her legendary gift of putting people at their ease, instinctively recognizing any hesitation or embarrassment, was a wonderful help to her as Queen, and later as the Queen Mother. This trait has endeared her to millions of people all over the world who have been fortunate enough to meet her.

There was something infinitely touching in the sight of the young Prince Charles, placed between his grandmother, the Queen Mother, and his aunt, Princess Margaret, amid the pomp and ceremony of his mother's coronation. The machine of state rolls remorselessly forward and onlookers were aware that, one day, this little boy would be the leading figure at the next coronation.

CHARLES'S GIRLFRIENDS

In some ways, Charles has led a less restricted life than many previous Princes of Wales, although both his father, the Duke of Edinburgh, and great-uncle, Earl Mountbatten, ensured that he developed a fitting sense of duty and responsibility. The period he spent at Trinity College, Cambridge was one of the most relaxed and enjoyable of his youth.

Charles was given a much looser rein than any of his predecessors, but, nevertheless the pressures were very much there. As he moved into his twenties, Charles's name was romantically linked with a number of eligible girls – and not a few ineligible ones – especially by the more excitable sections of the popular press who also enjoyed greater freedom to speculate about royal romances than they had in the past.

Every new girlfriend – and, as a rich and personable bachelor he attracted more than a few – provoked a fresh fit of hysteria from the tabloids. At Cambridge, where he had been an undergraduate at Trinity College, he had had a brief friendship with Lucia Santa Cruz, a history student and daughter of the Chilean ambassador. Other girlfriends whose company he enjoyed included Sybilla Norman, daughter of the Governor-General of Malta, the two daughters of Lord Buxton, the naturalist and an old friend of his father's, Jane Ward, Anna Wallace and Sabrina Guinness. The long list of Charles's old flames included Lady Leonora Grosvenor, daughter of the Duke of Westminster and her sister Lady Jane, Lady Victoria Perry, daughter of the Duke of Northumberland, Bettina Lindsay, daughter of Lord Balniel, Lady Cecil Kerr, daughter of the

Marquis of Lothian, Lady Henrietta Fitzroy, daughter of the Duke of Rutland and her cousin Elizabeth Manners, Angela Nevill, daughter of Lord Nevill, Lady Camilla Fane, daughter of the Earl of Westmorland, Caroline Longman, daughter of the publisher Mark Longman, Louise Astor, daughter of Lord Astor, Georgina Russell, daughter of Sir John Russell, and Rosie Chilton, daughter of an army colonel. No doubt this catalogue of well-born lovelies could be extended but it is probably no more extensive than could be made by any moneyed young man about town.

Prince Charles clearly enjoyed – and still enjoys – the company of women, but when it came to the really serious matter of a future wife and future Queen, the choice was more limited. There were few young women to whom Charles was truly and deeply attached and who were also acceptable for the public role of Princess of Wales and, later, Queen.

There was much speculation about Princess Marie-Astrid of Luxembourg, daughter of the ruler of the principality. But the Prince was not really interested, and, furthermore, she is a Roman Catholic, so there would be serious constitutional problems about such a marriage.

Charles was known to be very fond of Davina Sheffield, daughter of a distinguished army officer, and was seen in her company – and very evidently enjoying it – many times. He was even photographed arm-in-arm with her, a unique sign of Princely approval and affection. However, just when Charles was most deeply involved with Davina, a boorish and jealous ex-fiancé revealed that he and Davina had once lived together as man and wife. This was the effective end of the affair.

Lady Jane Wellesley, the daughter of the Duke of Wellington, was another firm favourite for a long time. Her pedigree was impeccable, and she was both beautiful and clever. During 1973 and 1974 she endured a permanent escort of photographers and reporters. There were constant rumours of an impending engagement and when she was invited to Sandringham for a weekend as a guest of the Queen, speculation reached fever pitch: no less than 10,000 people turned up to witness her arrival and departure. There were rumours that Charles had proposed to her and that she had refused him. It is more likely that, as Charles was about to start his career in the armed forces, he was not seriously considering marriage at the time.

Camilla Shand, the niece of Lord Ashcombe, was another of his great favourites. A girl of great character, highly intelligent, articulate and attractive, she shared many of his interests. She joined courage to her other qualities and was able to keep up with him on the hunting field on many occasions. He appeared to be deeply in love with her and she with him, and mutual friends believed that they would have made an excellent royal couple. Again, nothing came of it and eventually Camilla married a dashing cavalry officer, Andrew Parker-Bowles. Apparently Charles missed her company, but they remain good friends: Charles is godfather to their son Thomas.

Last and most interesting of all his really close girl-friends was Diana's elder sister Sarah. The Queen invited her to a house party at Windsor during Ascot week in the summer of 1977. Charles was immediately attracted to this red-haired, lively young woman, and they were soon much in each other's company, especially at sporting events. They spent a ten-day skiing holiday in Switzerland with the Duke of Gloucester's party, and the press began to take serious notice of Sarah Spencer. But, contrary to appearances and speculation, Sarah was never in love with Charles and viewed him as a friendly, brotherly figure. Finally,

In spite of much press speculation about a possible romance, Prince Charles and Lady Sarah Spencer were 'just good friends'. They shared common interests and enjoyed each other's company, but were not destined to spend their lives together.

exasperated by constant press persecution, she said plainly: 'He is fabulous as a person but I am not in love with him. He is a romantic who falls in love easily but I can assure you that if there were to be any engagement between Prince Charles and myself it would have happened by now. I am a whirlwind sort of lady as opposed to a person who goes in for long, slow-developing courtships. Of course, the Prince and I are great friends, but I was with him in Switzerland because of my skiing ability. Our relationship is totally platonic. I do not believe the Prince wants to marry yet. He has still not met the person he wants to marry. I think of him as the big brother I never had. I wouldn't marry anyone I didn't love, whether it was a dustman or the King of England. If he asked me, I would turn him down.'

This statement definitively ended any romance there might have been. But, in fact, Sarah was mistaken. Prince Charles had met the person he wanted to marry, although he was not aware of it at the time. It happened at a shoot at Althorp to which Sarah had invited Charles in November 1977. Diana was also there. Charles noticed that Sarah had a sister. She was, Charles later noted, 'a very amusing and jolly – and attractive 16-year-old'.

FALLING IN LOVE

When Diana came to live in London at the age of 17 after her abrupt departure from Switzerland and her father's serious illness, Charles heard about it and asked her out occasionally, usually to make up a party. She was obviously too young at this time to engage his serious interest, but she was good company. He asked her to the theatre, the ballet, and to meals. She was, after all, the little sister of his current girl friend.

As Diana passed from her seventeenth into her eighteenth year, she began to blossom from a fresh-faced schoolgirl into an attractive young woman. Charles found himself looking at her with very different eyes. In her eyes, he had not changed: she had seen him at close quarters with a succession of girl friends, including her own sister. She was in love with him, and now, suddenly, he was looking at her in a new light.

On his thirtieth birthday Prince Charles announced that he was now seriously looking for the wife he, his mother and the whole world knew he needed. While

When Diana returned to London after spending part of the New Year holiday with the Royal Family at Sandringham, newspaper stories reached a new level of hysteria. Throughout January and February 1981, photographs of her appeared almost every day. We now know that Charles proposed to Diana in January 1981, but the announcement was not made until the following month. Throughout this trying time, Diana behaved with extraordinary discretion and diplomacy.

by no means desperate, he was very much on the lookout for a suitable future Queen. Diana was obviously responsive and he began to see her qualities more clearly. He started to take her out more often. The Queen, too, must have begun to have similar thoughts at the same time because in August 1979, when Diana was just 18, the Queen asked her to join a royal house party at Balmoral. There Diana enjoyed renewing her childhood friendship with Prince Andrew. In February 1980 she was asked to join the Royal Family at Sandringham, near her old home at Park House. In July, Charles invited her to watch him play in a polo match in Cunex. A couple of weeks later she joined the Royal Family on the royal yacht *Britannia* at Cowes.

In the first week of September she went north to Balmoral to visit Charles and on this occasion, a photographer with a long-range camera and a lot of luck photographed her fishing with him on the River Dee. By this time, the world's press had realized that something serious was afoot and that this shy young woman was more than an accidental guest at these meetings. Public excitement intensified; it seemed that the whole country was at fever pitch to know if rumour was right and Lady Diana would marry the popular heir to the throne.

Relations between Fleet Street (traditional home of the British newspaper industry) and the Palace hit an all-time low in 1980. A motion was even tabled in the House of Commons deploring the media's treatment of Diana.

Many expected an announcement to be made on the Prince's birthday in November, but this was not forthcoming. In fact, he now embarked upon a long-arranged three-week trip to the Indian sub-continent.

By now the couple had been exploring their feelings for each other. Diana had been in love with Charles for three years, and now Charles was falling in love with her. But he knew better than she did the enormous strain that would be put on her, not only when their engagement was announced but for the rest of her life. Her future as Princess of Wales and then Queen was going to be a very public one. But 'love conquers all' and Diana made it clear that she would willingly accept the challenge.

Apart from these publicly known meetings, the couple managed some private meetings at the Queen Mother's home in Scotland, but by now the world's press was in full cry. They had soon discovered where Diana lived and worked and they laid a siege to both. Quite suddenly she was thrust into the full glare of universal publicity. Overnight, she changed from an unknown young woman to one of the world's most famous media figures. Every meeting with Charles was now followed by headlines and speculative articles. Her background, her family, her friends were subjected to the minutest scrutiny and when the press could not find a story, they made up one. Relations between the Royal Family and Fleet Street touched rock bottom.

Diana, not surprisingly, found the press invasion of every corner of her life unnerving, but she managed to preserve her calmness and good humour under the most difficult circumstances. However, sometimes even her spirit quailed. On one occasion in late November, the Press Association put out a story about a supposed interview where she was quoted as saying she would like to marry soon. Next day she wept as she denied the story, but the PA refused to withdraw it.

Diana's mother, remembering her own ordeal during her divorce, was finally moved to write a letter to *The Times*. It read: 'In recent weeks many articles have been labelled "exclusive quotes" when the plain truth is that my daughter has not spoken the words attributed to her. Fanciful speculation, if it is in good taste, is one thing, but this can be embarrassing. Lies are quite another matter, and by their nature, hurtful and inexcusable... May I ask the editors of Fleet Street whether, in the execution of their jobs, they consider it necessary or fair to harass my daughter daily from dawn till well after dusk? Is it fair to ask any human being, regardless of circumstance, to be treated in this way? The freedom of the press was granted by law, by public demand, for very good reasons. But when these privileges are abused, can the press command any respect, or expect to be shown any respect?'

No less than 60 MPs put down a motion in the House of Commons which deplored 'the manner in which Lady Diana Spencer is treated by the media' and called upon 'those responsible to have more concern for individual privacy'. There was also an unprecedented meeting between Press Council members and Fleet Street editors to see what could be done about the situation. There was some improvement, but nothing could stop the intense speculation in the newspapers and magazines, not only in Britain but all over the world. When Charles and Diana met at Sandringham on New Year's Day, having spent Christmas with their respective families, the press was there in full strength. Charles finally lost his temper. 'I should like to take this opportunity,' he snapped, 'to wish you all a very happy New Year and your editors a particularly nasty one.'

THE ENGAGEMENT

After lunch with the Queen and Prince Andrew, Charles and Diana were interviewed – and, of course, photographed – on the steps of Buckingham Palace on the day their engagement was finally announced.

In January 1981, in his apartments at Buckingham Palace, Charles formally asked Diana to marry him. She accepted at once: she had never wavered in her love for him and her desire to be his wife. She was about to leave on an Australian holiday with her mother and stepfather and Charles wanted her to have time to think the whole thing through. But Diana had no doubts.

On Tuesday, 24 February, 1981, at 1 pm, Michael O'Shea, the Queen's Press Secretary, issued an official statement to the Press Association. It read simply, 'It is with the greatest pleasure that the Queen and the Duke of Edinburgh announce the betrothal of their beloved son, the Prince of Wales, to Lady Diana Spencer, daughter of the Earl Spencer and the Honourable Mrs Shand-Kydd.'

From now on Diana's life would be utterly changed – the £30,000 oval sapphire surrounded by 14 diamonds and set in 18 carat gold was the outward and visible symbol of that. From now on she was accepted into the Royal Family, with all that this implied.

On the great day, the newly engaged couple had a quiet lunch with the Queen and Prince Andrew, who was on leave from the Royal Navy, and then stood on the steps of Buckingham Palace to be photographed and interviewed by the world's press. Diana obliged the photographers by twisting her beautiful ring this way and that so that everyone could get a good picture. 'Are you in love?' shouted one impertinent newsman. 'Of course!' said Diana immediately and happily. 'Whatever in love means', said Charles more characteristically. They were questioned about the age gap; after all Charles was 33 and Diana was still only 19. 'I've never really thought about it,' said Diana. 'You're only as young as you think you are,' replied Charles rather more obscurely. 'Diana will certainly keep me young!'

After all the chasing, the rat-pack of journalists following Diana's every move, and the siege of her flat and school, this final and formal press conference at the end of the courtship must have been a truly happy and relaxing occasion.

Diana, of course, could never return to her flat. From now on she was truly public property, like everyone else in the Royal Family. No more driving in her beloved Metro; from now on, it would be chauffeured rides in the royal Rolls Royce, and always with her own personal detective. In fact, from now on she would never on any occasion be by herself in public again. This 'girl-next-door' who had shopped in supermarkets, waited in queues for buses, and driven round the streets of London looking for a parking space, had radically changed her lifestyle and her future.

For her first few days as Princess-in-waiting, Diana stayed with the Queen Mother at Clarence House. Her grandmother, Lady Fermoy, one of the Queen Mother's Ladies-in-Waiting and an old friend, was also there, no doubt with much affectionate and useful advice on the many complications of the new life ahead. Shortly after this, she moved into a suite at Buckingham Palace to await her wedding day.

There was not only a trousseau to be planned, but clothes suitable for countless public engagements had to be selected. Her mother was there to guide

The Queen Mother was the ideal person to guide and counsel Diana as she approached her new role and royal responsibilities. She herself had been plunged into the role of Queen Consort, and had a lifetime of unmatched experience on which to draw.

her and, as both her sisters had worked on *Vogue* magazine, the fashion and beauty editors gave her some invaluable advice. Like many tall women, Lady Diana had a tendency to drop her head when she walked: another editor and former model was able to give her some useful hints on facing cameras and crowds. Other advice was given on how to cope with poise in a dozen or more situations such as how to get out of a car or helicopter with dignity. Her hairdresser tried out new styles, and the most comfortable way to wear a tiara. Some of her own fun jewellery, especially earrings, was specially adapted to take real diamonds, for now fabulous gems were required to set off her new wardrobe. Prince Charles gave his fiancée a charm bracelet. Each charm has special significance, such as the wombat he added, when Prince William was born.

The first venture as an officially engaged couple was at Clarence House where they had a family dinner with both their grandparents. When they left, a large crowd greeted them with congratulatory cheers. Then a punishing round of public appearances began, but at last they were together and could support each other. Lady Diana's name appeared on court circulars and the wheels for the wedding were put in motion. There was much to do: meetings with dressmakers and the great decision about The Dress. Diana needed a secretarial staff to deal with the thousands of letters that began to pour in, and Oliver Everett, an assistant private secretary to Prince Charles and an experienced diplomat, moved in to oversee this new and unfamiliar operation for her.

Deciding the date of the wedding needed much discussion because it would be a great national and international event and there were many considerations to be taken into account. The date was fixed for 29 July and it was announced that it would be a public holiday. It was also announced that the wedding would take place at St Paul's Cathedral, a break with royal tradition; Westminster Abbey has been the usual venue for royal weddings in the twentieth century.

Diana's first official public engagement was on 9 March – a recital at Goldsmith's Hall in London in aid of the Royal Opera House Development Appeal. Princess Grace of Monaco was among those taking part. The former film star had much to talk over with the future Princess. A large crowd had gathered outside to greet the couple as they arrived and left. Diana chose to wear a daring, black, taffeta strapless dress to the great delight of the photographers. It was obvious that the world of fashion had acquired a brilliant new star.

'Shy Diana' took the world by surprise
– and by storm – at her first public
engagement, when she appeared in a
stunning, black taffeta evening dress
designed by David and Elizabeth
Emanuel. This sophisticated, strapless
gown was the first indication of her
revolutionary approach to royal style.

After this glittering occasion there was a reception attended by about 300 distinguished guests. The universal view was that Diana was supremely happy as Charles's future wife. A small but happy touch is typical of Diana's grace and spontaneity. When she was presented with a single pink rose she immediately put it in her new fiancé's buttonhole, to his smiling approval.

Many more engagements followed in quick succession. In a helicopter piloted by the Prince, he and his fiancée paid an official visit this time to the headquarters of the Gloucestershire police at Cheltenham. This is the force responsible for their safety at Charles's new country home at Highgrove House, Tetbury. (He had acquired the estate from Maurice Macmillan the previous year and this in itself had resulted in a fresh burst of press speculation about his matrimonial plans.) It was – and remains – the couple's first home.

They toured the police headquarters and even found time to visit the stables and meet the horses, Prince Charles's favourite animals. As they left, a boy in the crowd offered Lady Diana, or Lady Di as she was increasingly called, a single daffodil and asked her if he could kiss her hand. She smilingly accepted. She has always been good at this sort of natural gesture and gives ordinary people extraordinary pleasure.

The list of engagements seemed endless but, in the meantime, the necessary wheels of state began to grind their inexorable way. The Queen convened a special meeting of the Privy Council to obtain their formal consent to the marriage. It was also necessary to consult the Archbishop of Canterbury, the Moderator of the General Assembly of the Church of Scotland and other religious leaders as Charles would one day be 'Defender of the Faith'.

Protocol demanded that Prince Charles should seek the Queen's consent to his marriage, and that Her Majesty should convene a meeting of the Privy Council to obtain their formal consent. The special licence for the marriage was on view in the sanctuary at Westminster Abbey.

The logistics of the wedding itself needed careful planning. How many bridesmaids and who would be given this unique honour? The answer in this case was five, led by Lady Sarah Armstrong-Jones, daughter of Princess Margaret and cousin to Prince Charles. The others were India Hicks, granddaughter of Lord Louis Mountbatten, Sarah Jane Caselet, daughter of the trainer of Prince Charles's race horses, Catherine Cameron, the daughter of Donald Cameron of Lochiel, and Clementine Hambro, the great grand-daughter of Winston Churchill. The pages would be Lord Nicholas Windsor, son of the Duke and Duchess of Kent, and Edward van Cutsem, son of Mr and Mrs Hugh Cutsem. As was the royal custom, Prince Charles would not have a best man, but two supporters, his brothers Prince Andrew and Prince Edward.

The wedding cake would be made by the Royal Naval Cookery School at HMS *Pembroke* at Chatham.

The Lord Chamberlain was in charge of overall arrangements, as he had been when Princess Anne and Captain Mark Phillips were married at Westminster Abbey in November 1973. The wedding, however, was to be on a much vaster scale with worldwide television coverage for an estimated 750 million viewers. A small ferret called Nipper was used to pull cable through pipes for the television pictures. Guests would include royalty and heads of state, and the long processional route would be lined by servicemen, the ever-present security men checking with dogs and helicopters and marksmen on the rooftops. The timing of the procession had to be carefully worked out – often early in the morning before the streets were busy with the traffic that would be missing on the actual day.

In the meantime, life for the engaged couple went on. For the next four months there was an exceptionally busy schedule. At the end of March, Charles left on a long-arranged tour of New Zealand, Australia, Venezuela and the United States. This could not be changed, nor could Diana be included at this stage. She saw him off at Heathrow Airport with tears in her eyes; she did not see him again until he returned in May. In the meantime, their only contact with each other was by telephone.

Not that Diana was not busy during his absence. She visited the Queen at Windsor on Her Majesty's fifty-fifth birthday. There were all the arrangements for her wedding dress, her trousseau to be bought and the necessity for her to practise walking with a long and awkward train behind her. This she did by pinning a long sheet to her shoulders.

Prince Charles flew back from the United States on 3 May. He landed at the RAF base at Lossiemouth and drove straight to Balmoral, where an anxious Lady Diana was waiting for him. Here they were able to spend a few days holiday in each other's company and Prince Charles and Diana went fishing on the River Dee. Now, also, as happens to every engaged couple, the wedding presents began to arrive and had to be looked at, noted and suitable letters of thanks composed and sent.

When this short break was over it was back to a busy round of royal engagements, some separately, but mostly together. In early May they visited Broadlands, the Hampshire home of the late Lord Louis Mountbatten who had been assassinated in 1979 and whom Charles still mourned. They opened a commemorative exhibition there, and Diana planted her first tree, a traditional royal occupation that she was soon to become used to.

May also saw the Prince and his fiancée at a lunch in honour of the President of Ghana at Windsor. The same afternoon Lady Diana was there when the Queen

Early in their engagement, Charles had to leave Diana for an extensive tour of Australasia and the United States. On his return, the young couple took a brief holiday at Balmoral. An expert fisherman, Charles was landing salmon upstream, while Diana took lessons from the head ghillie.

Members of the Royal Family are frequently called upon to plant trees. Diana had her first experience of this unique version of arboriculture when she and Charles visited Broadlands, home of the late Earl Mountbatten, and the house where they would be spending their wedding night.

presented their new colours to the 1st Battalion of the Welsh Guards of which Prince Charles is Colonel-in-Chief. Diana was a guest at two state banquets given in honour of King Khaled of Saudi Arabia on his state visit, the first given by the Queen at Buckingham Palace, the second given by the King at Claridges. From her earliest days, Diana was given lessons by both observation and example, as to how a queen conducts herself on great state occasions.

Both Prince Charles and Lady Diana had to visit St Paul's Cathedral to listen to the music to be played at the wedding itself. In fact, the music was one of the finest of many splendid features of this magnificent occasion and included, at Prince Charles's special request, Kiri Te Kanawa, the New Zealand soprano. Then they lunched with the Archbishop of Canterbury to discuss the details of the wedding. Here it was decided that Diana would say 'love, honour and cherish' rather than the more old-fashioned 'love, honour and obey'.

In June, Diana attended Trooping the Colour, the ceremony that celebrates the Queen's official birthday, and she watched her fiancé take part as Colonel-in-Chief of the Welsh Guards. It was on this occasion that a young man in the crowd fired blank shots as the Queen approached, but Her Majesty controlled her horse with amazing skill and rode on, pale but composed. As a Lady of a Knight Companion of the Order, Lady Diana attended the Order of the Garter Service of Thanksgiving at St George's Chapel, Windsor. This was followed by her attendance at Royal Ascot and her first ride in an open carriage. She was very much the centre of attention and wildly cheered by the large crowd which lined the rails to see the royal procession drive past. She was now one of the world media superstars. Ascot week ended with a belated twenty-first birthday party for Prince Andrew at Windsor. The birthday itself had been in February, just before the announcement of his brother's engagement.

The last days of her nineteenth year saw two more public appearances for Diana. The first was a service at the Royal Academy of Arts and the second a gala première of the James Bond film *For Your Eyes Only* at the Odeon, Leicester Square. This exhausting week was ended by an attendance at a military music pageant at Wembley.

The day before Diana's twentieth birthday, Prince Charles hosted a garden party at his Gloucestershire home of Highgrove. The guests were tenants from his estates in the Duchy of Cornwall. Diana's birthday itself, on 15 July, was celebrated quietly with family and a few friends. The wedding day was now fast approaching.

One of Diana's pleasures is playing tennis at a private club in London. Wimbledon saw no less than three visits by Diana, including the women's singles final. Not all the events she had to attend were ceremonial bores!

During these final days, the first official portrait of Lady Diana by Bryan Organ, Prince Charles's favourite portrait painter, was hung at the National Portrait Gallery. It immediately attracted large crowds. Commemorative stamps to mark the wedding were issued and guests began to arrive in large numbers, the Prince played his final two pre-nuptial games of polo at Windsor and Cowdray Park and there were the last rehearsals at St Paul's, the final dress fittings — and the usual private stag party for Prince Charles.

The Queen Mother gave her grandson's future wife hints on how to meet a host of people and to keep smiling, however bored or tired she might feel or however much her interest was flagging. She must remember that meeting her was probably the most exciting event in the lives of many ordinary people who often waited hours for the privilege.

The first official portrait of Diana was painted by Bryan Organ and provoked considerable controversy and argument about whether it did justice to her sparkling good looks.

THE WEDDING

It was a unique occasion on 23 July when Prince Charles and Lady Diana were interviewed at Buckingham Palace by Angela Rippon and Andrew Gardener for BBC Television. Diana endeared herself to parents by publicly thanking all the small children who had sent her presents of cakes they had made specially for her, many decorated with Smarties!

The wedding celebrations started on the night of 28 July, with a huge firework display in London's Hyde Park. Hundreds of thousands of people thronged the park to watch the fantastic show.

The eve of the wedding saw the biggest fireworks display for over 200 years take place in Hyde Park. Half a million people gathered to enjoy the show and to ensure themselves good places on the wedding route the following day. Behind the scenes an enormous security operation had taken place and there were tracker dogs, police marksmen on strategic rooftops, all the paraphernalia of a top-level occasion. Nothing could be left to chance. All was now ready.

The wedding of Lady Diana Spencer and Prince Charles in July 1981 was a fairytale occasion. As Diana rode in the glass coach from Clarence House to St Paul's (above) she was surrounded by a sea of cheering crowds, eager to welcome the soon-to-be Princess and to catch a glimpse of her fabulous wedding gown. It was the first major public occasion when Diana was the centre of attention and she carried it off with truly regal grace and aplomb. As she left the cathedral on her new husband's arm (left), she looked every inch the Princess she had just become.

The Prince and Princess of Wales drove in an open coach to Buckingham Palace along the Mall (above). Crowds of well-wishers lined the route and cheered the radiantly smiling and waving bride. Diana's wedding dress (right) was a closely guarded secret until the day itself. Designed by David and Elizabeth Emanuel, it was a dreamy creation in silk taffeta with a 25-foot long, lace-edged court train. The bridesmaids' charming dresses complemented hers, and their delightful coronets of flowers harmonized with her traditional bouquet.

The royal advisers had guessed well, or were lucky, or both, in choosing the day for the wedding all those months before. July 29, 1981 dawned bright and sunny with blue skies and no danger of rain. Lady Diana had stayed the night at Clarence House, home of the Queen Mother and her carriage was to follow shortly behind the others.

The guests arrived in their state cars and had taken their places in St Paul's when the royal procession finally left Buckingham Palace with their escorts from the Household Cavalry. The carriages contained the Duke and Duchess of Kent, Prince and Princess Michael of Kent, Princess Alexandra and her husband, the Honourable Angus Ogilvie, the Duke and Duchess of Gloucester, Princess Anne and Captain Mark Phillips, Princess Margaret, the Queen Mother and, finally the Queen and the Duke of Edinburgh. Then Prince Charles appeared in the uniform of a naval Commander, with his brother Prince Andrew in the uniform of a midshipman and carrying the precious ring. The final carriage left the palace at 10.30 am.

Then, most important of all, the glass coach carrying the bride left Clarence House on its way to the Cathedral. The fairytale princess was about to become a real Princess. The dress, one of enchantment and romance, with Tudor, Victorian and Edwardian influences in its design (by David and Elizabeth Emanuel) was perfect for the bride. The ivory silk taffeta crinoline shimmered as the sunlight glittered on the embroidered, 25-foot long train. The bouquet, (which by royal custom, started by the Queen Mother after her marriage in 1923) was later taken to rest upon the Tomb of the Unknown Warrior in Westminster Abbey. It was made up of lily-of-the-valley, Mountbatten roses, freesias, stephanotis, orchids, and ivy, with traditional bridal myrtle and veronica. Queen Victoria carried myrtle from a bush at Osborne House at her wedding.

Firmly grasping her father's arm, each giving strength to the other, the veiled bride, to the accompaniment of the *Trumpet Voluntary* began the three-and-a-half-minute walk up the aisle. Earl Spencer, who has never totally recovered from his stroke, had a perceptible limp, but he played his part bravely, although he had to be assisted to his seat by his son.

The Archbishop conducted the service and both the bride and groom made nervous but understandable errors in their wedding vows. The crowd went wild when they finally emerged as man and wife and the journey back to the palace in an open landau was a continuous triumph. The happy Prince and Princess appeared on the balcony with other members of the Royal Family and Charles gave Diana the famous kiss. The crowd went mad.

They spent their wedding night at Broadlands and then relaxed for a few more days before flying off to Gibraltar to join the royal yacht *Britannia* for a Mediterranean cruise on which they combined the wonders of the pyramids with a visit to President Sadat of Egypt. A fortnight later they flew home to Scotland to begin their new life together.

Her marriage to Prince Charles was the first great public occasion when Diana herself was the central figure. However vivid the accounts of previous royal weddings she had read, however detailed the rehearsals, the impact of the drive through crowded and cheering streets, the cathedral packed with world statesmen and great dignitaries, the solemnity and grandeur of the occasion itself, the fanfares, flags and bunting — and all of it for her — must have been overwhelming for a girl hardly out of her teens. Certainly, it must have been the first great leap forward in the making of a Queen.

Charles and Diana left for their honeymoon in an open carriage to which younger members of the Royal Family had tied balloons and good luck symbols. Diana's going-away outfit (an essential item in any bride's trousseau) was a striking shade of coral with a saucy plumed hat.

CHAPTER 3
THE
NEW
PRINCESS

When Lady Diana Spencer walked into St Paul's on the arm of her father on 29 July, 1981, she walked in as an essentially private person. When she walked out on the arm of her husband, she was essentially a public figure. From then on she was the future Queen of the realm and this fact would determine everything she did. The transformation would be total. She would never be by herself in public again; her life would be ruled by formal protocol. She had, in fact, become a public icon rather than a young woman of normal needs and inclinations. As Princess of Wales she now had a role which had more in common with unending theatre than with the common daily life with all its vagaries and accidents, its good and bad luck. She had a part to play and she could never afford to fluff her lines.

All roles need learning and rehearsal, and the story of Diana's education into royalty was in one sense very lengthy and in another extremely short and concentrated. The long stage of her education started the day she was born into one of the country's oldest and most aristocratic families. From birth she was surrounded by servants and all the care and attention that money could buy. From her earliest days she saw around her the way a great house and estate is run. She learned how to handle domestic staff unselfconsciously and to recognize the rare occasions when it is permissible to unbend and show that she too is an imperfect and vulnerable human being. And, of course, she came from a family with a long history of service and friendship with the crown. She was a real Lady too, with a title in her own right.

Being a rich and well brought-up young woman of a noble family does not necessarily qualify someone to be the Queen and consort of His Britannic Majesty of the United Kingdom of Great Britain and Northern Ireland. Undoubtedly, when it became clear to the Royal Family that the 32-year old Prince had serious intentions towards Lady Diana, royal heads were put together very quickly.

Previous page: Diana blossomed with marriage and quickly acquired both poise and grace, without sacrificing either her sincerity or her warmth.

Right: A warm friendship developed between the Queen Mother and Diana during their time together at Clarence House before the wedding. The Queen Mother occupies a very special place in the hearts of the nation and, with her guidance, Diana, too, has created her own unique niche.

Below: Wherever she goes Diana is 'public property' – almost an icon. When the young couple toured the Far East, huge posters were displayed on main roads.

51

THE QUEEN MOTHER

The most important advisers on Diana's future role were the Queen Mother and her good friend and Lady-in-Waiting, Lady Fermoy. (Lady Fermoy is also Diana's grandmother.) These two distinguished women between them knew more about royal protocol than a roomful of historians, equerries, and experts. Queen Elizabeth had been a queen since 1937, and there can be few royal situations with which she is not totally familiar. Her years as Queen Consort took her to every corner of the world: she has met presidents, emperors, and every other kind of head of state. The world's greatest and most famous men and women have bowed or curtsied to her. As Queen Mother she has undertaken a ferocious schedule of public appearances and, by the time Diana appeared on the world stage, she had become the beloved mother of the nation. In the making of a new queen, no one could exceed her experience and authority.

Lady Fermoy's family on both sides has a long history and experience of royal service. She herself, as the intimate friend of the Queen Mother, knows to the finest degree the lines that can and cannot be crossed. She knows how to judge a curtsey to the millimetre, how to shake a royal hand or kiss a royal cheek, when to stay and offer human sympathy, and when to withdraw to allow royal tears to flow in solitude. Lady Fermoy, in fact, has become the perfect royal friend and confidante.

The two of them together must have made a formidable educational machine for Diana. But it was not frightening because Diana knew them both and would listen attentively. She knew that they cared for her as a relative and as a person rather than just a girl who was to marry the Prince of Wales. When the engagement was announced and Diana went to stay at Clarence House, the two old friends were waiting for her. They knew that they had a most important and serious teaching job on their hands.

When it came to describing the facts of public life, Charles had explained, in his own particular way and from his own masculine viewpoint, some of the difficulties that Diana would face as Princess of Wales. In fact, before he proposed and when they were sensibly discussing the considerable 'ifs' and 'buts' of her being married to the Prince and future King, he tried to explain to her the sheer awfulness of a dedicated public life. But it was obviously a 'hopeless' task; Diana was a young woman in love and was prepared to make any sacrifice to be with the man she loved. In addition he was a man and 32 years old; how could he know how a girl just over half his age would feel and react?

The Queen Mother is a different case entirely. Charles has spent his entire life in the public eye. From babyhood and childhood, through his presentation to the people as Prince of Wales, his schooling in Scotland and Australia, his years as an undergraduate at Trinity College, Cambridge, through his service as a soldier, an RAF pilot, and a naval officer, his life as a sportsman, his day-to-day visits and speeches as a leading royal figure – all of these parts have been played in the full gaze of the public eye. His grandmother, however, had no such lifelong preparation for the royal spotlight. She had married a shy nervous man who had chosen the comparatively quiet existence of a country squire and naval officer before the abdication of his older brother catapulted him and his wife into the continuous harsh glare of royal life. She knows very well the enormous difference this made to her – and the changes that marriage would make to the innocent young girl about to join the Royal Family.

As the new Princess of Wales, Diana relied on her husband for advice on how she should tackle her public role, but Charles would not have been able to put himself mentally in Diana's position to the same extent as the Queen Mother could. Public ceremony and royal responsibility have always been part of his life. Even as a very young man he was able to take events such as his investiture at Caernarvon Castle in 1969 in his stride.

The Queen Mother and Lady Fermoy must have had many conversations about the past and the future as they oversaw and gently encouraged Charles's courtship of Diana. The Queen Mother is a woman of the world, too. She has daughters of her own and knows how difficult it is for young royal lovers to find private time by themselves away from the over-zealous attentions of reporters and photographers. So she lent them her house in Scotland for part of their courtship. She undoubtedly recalled, although the context was very different, the extra distress and additional strain that publicity placed on the entire Royal Family and on her younger daughter in particular during Princess Margaret's doomed romance with Group Captain Peter Townsend.

Diana's education as a 'royal' began at Clarence House. Apart from anything else, she needed to learn how to avoid making serious mistakes. For example, the Queen herself has learned to be marvellously adept at moving gracefully through the sensitive minefields of politics. With the media avid to pick up the slightest hint of political preference or prejudice, she has always appeared to be totally impartial, although as an intelligent, informed and spirited woman there must have been times when governments of both colours have disappointed or angered her.

Diana had had no training in making her way through this minefield. It was no help to say to her 'steer clear of politics and don't make any loaded political remarks', when a seemingly simple phrase like 'I'm sorry for poor people' or 'We've always had a good army' could be given a sinister political significance it was never intended to bear. For a 19-year-old, this complex world of power politics must have been a frightening place, full of hidden traps.

This was the world to which the Queen Mother and Lady Fermoy gently introduced her. At the same time they avoided making her suspicious or over-wary. There is a fine line to be walked between credulity and mistrust, and Diana had to find and walk it with confidence and assurance. She did not have much time to learn this lesson. From the day the engagement was announced, everything she said, every gesture she made, every smile or frown she bestowed was immediately and minutely dissected. She was no longer simply a pretty girl having a chat; she was a future queen expressing a specific, political view, or, at least, she could be made to appear so. The press is not always kind, scrupulous or, in some cases, even truthful in these matters.

No one will ever know – because none of the three participants will ever say – what exactly was said at this time, but the lessons were successful because in the intervening years Diana has been careful to say nothing that could be twisted and used against her, Prince Charles or royalty in general. In fact, Diana, in all the roles she has undertaken, has been a major influence in maintaining the relevance of the monarchy to contemporary life. She is not seen as a remote and austere royal being, but as a warm and lively young woman, interested in many of the things that interest ordinary people.

Undoubtedly Diana listened with the closest possible attention and the two older women would have ensured that the awesome prospect of future queenship made the necessary deep impression on her. But at the end of the day, it would have been the example of the Queen Mother and her long history of public life that must have made the most lasting impression. To have got it exactly right, both as Queen Consort and later as Queen Mother, for over 50 years was the most compelling example an inexperienced young woman could have hoped for. There, in the living, smiling flesh was the epitome of successful queen consortship in modern times.

Diana already had friends and allies in the Royal Family even before her marriage. She and Prince Andrew are close in age and have been companions since childhood.

Diana has made few mistakes in the process of learning to be a Princess and is likely to make even fewer in learning to be a Queen. She has absorbed her 'lessons' quickly and thoroughly and is proving to be a real asset to the House of Windsor.

THE ROYAL FAMILY

The Queen herself, while perfectly friendly, did not have the time to instruct her future daughter-in-law in the finer points of queenship. As all her family and close advisers have discovered, she has a number of ways of displaying royal displeasure. There is no evidence that Diana has ever been at the sharp end of such treatment, but certainly she will have observed the Queen's way of doing things as another model for her future role.

The other immediate members of the Royal Family are a different matter. From childhood, Diana has been on friendly terms with Prince Andrew, and they had corresponded while she was at school. He would have been anxious to do what he could to help and, being close in age to Diana, could offer some forthright views on the people she would meet. These brotherly tips must have been very useful when she was finding her way through a sea of new faces.

Princess Anne, too, would have been helpful. She would have an idea of what it must be like for a relatively unsophisticated girl to be plunged into the unfamiliar strait-jacket of court protocol with its rules of etiquette and forms of address, who stands and who sits down where and when, when to speak first and when to wait to be spoken to, what kind of clothes to wear on what occasions.

This rigidity of protocol is no accident. These affairs need to be regulated, not only in the cause of domestic harmony, but, most importantly, in the Palace's external relations. Where the arrival and departure of people – ambassadors, prime ministers, world statesmen, political leaders – is a daily occurrence, the need for absolute consistency is paramount. No ambassador, from the tiniest principality to the mightiest state, must be made to feel more or less important than any other ambassador. No person, however important or unimportant, must leave the Palace with the feeling that he or she has been treated without perfect courtesy and consideration. This is the function of protocol - to make sure that nothing can go wrong. It is no easy matter for a young girl used to the normal give-and-take of family life, the squabbles, laughter, and tears that go to make up the pattern of existence for most of us to adapt to the formal rigidities of the royal court.

Her husband-to-be was the person Diana would lean on most heavily during this formative period of her royal life. We know he had many earnest discussions with her, pointing out all the disadvantages of being his wife, the heavy burden of responsibility from which she could never escape, and the duties which would never fall from her shoulders. He would have stressed that the media pressure would get worse, not better, and that the press would take an intrusive and prurient interest in their most private and intimate moments together.

Diana quickly discovered the danger of the media. The development of accurate telescopic lenses for cameras meant that unguarded moments could be caught at long distance. Fanatical papparazzi who had penetrated the security net would lurk hidden in the undergrowth a mile away, almost totally out of sight, and snap away to their hearts' delight. The pregnant Diana in a bikini, caught by such a photographic storm-trooper, appeared in less scrupulous tabloids across the world and caused her understandable distress. So, even after she had joined the Royal Family, Diana still had things to learn.

As Princess of Wales, Diana had to get used to another phenomenon – her personal staff. This includes a senior adviser, appointed by the Palace, who is responsible for the secretarial staff and who looks after her diary. In fact, her first four days as fiancée of the Prince of Wales produced a flood of letters from all over the world, all of which needed to be answered.

She also has several Ladies-in-Waiting. This unpaid job is a high honour and not without its onerous duties. In the first instance, Ladies-in-Waiting were appointed by the Palace with due regard to their experience of royal household protocol and the extreme youth of the Princess. They would have given her all the essential tips about what to avoid to survive in public life: how to get in and out of helicopters without showing too much leg, how to avoid crunchy or flaky food, and so on.

So Diana's crash course in royalty had to be both wide and deep. Obviously, she learned both quickly and well and soon became a highly experienced public figure, disguising any boredom she might feel, showing interest in a most professional manner. Her ready smile and the breathtaking array of beautiful clothes have made her a world leader of fashion. Behind the glittering facade, however, there is still a responsive and vulnerable human being. No one could forget the shy, warm smile, the readiness to laugh at herself and her predicament, and her eyes, when she was besieged by the press during Charles's courtship. More than a decade of intense exposure to the public gaze has not destroyed that. Princess Di remains, in a way none of the other royals have managed to, a recognizably normal human being.

Life in the Royal Family may involve all kinds of considerations that would not occur to outsiders. Ladies-in-Waiting and other members of the royal household advise her on such things as dress conventions in host countries on foreign tours. In Saudi Arabia, for example, (right) Diana stayed cool without causing offence to Moslem traditions, whereas colourful clothes and lively informality wowed New York (below).

Most young women learn to get out of a car without showing too much leg, but helicopter travel requires a different technique (above). Diana has suffered more than any member of the Royal Family from intrusion into her privacy. In spite of the tightest security, she is still sometimes the victim of 'candid' photographs (left), which cause her unnecessary distress and embarrassment.

57

CHAPTER 4
THE
MIRROR
OF
FASHION

On the evening of 9 March, 1981 an event took place which was to revolutionize the world of fashion and give it a shock from which it has still not recovered. Simply, a young girl went to a recital in a black dress. Put less starkly, Lady Diana Spencer, the new fiancée of Charles, Prince of Wales, attended a poetry, prose and music recital at Goldsmiths' Hall, in London. It was her first public engagement in her new role. She wore a stunning off-the-shoulder black taffeta dress specially designed for the occasion by David and Elizabeth Emanuel.

It was an absolute sensation and the press made the most of it, splashing the front pages with big pictures and columns of print. The hard heads of the fashion world also sat up and took notice. They realized immediately that a new superstar had exploded into their universe, a superstar who would one day be Queen. The same day, off-the-shoulder black dresses were being designed and made in London, Paris, New York and the Far East, shortly to appear in the High Streets of cities across the world.

Previous page: Always smart and imaginative, Diana looked spectacular at the film première of the latest James Bond movie.

Below: Diana has a strong sense of individual style and, on her first public engagement, she set the keynote for a new era of royal fashion.

A SENSE OF STYLE

Diana's transformation into a leader of world fashion was instantaneous. From the black taffeta dress at Goldsmiths' Hall, it has been a march of stylistic triumph all the way. As the fashion expert Lesley Ebbetts writes:

Since her entry into the public glare in March 1981, she has perfectly dressed the part of the wife of the heir to the throne. She has done this while setting astonishing new precedents in royal dress for one so young... No Royal has taken so instantly to fashion trends, almost making them her own. No Royal before has used the advice of so many designers.

Diana does not seem to have been stylish or chic before her romance with Prince Charles. Like most country-bred girls, she favoured skirts, sweaters and scarves – the casual clothes worn by Sloane Rangers. She was a very pretty girl who wore her clothes well, but so were many others, and there were no early signs of the fashion megastar that lay hidden beneath the shy and demure exterior.

How did Diana engineer this astonishing transformation? What changed this shy fledgling into a bird of paradise? To begin with, she has a number of natural advantages. She is tall with an elegant figure, good bones, and an excellent physique. It is interesting that she has always been an excellent swimmer, a sport where co-ordination and grace are essential. Diana has no trouble at all with her physical co-ordination and never looks awkward.

Add to this natural gracefulness an obvious love of and delight in good clothes and the enthusiasm for seeking them out, and you have another essential ingredient in the making of the best-dressed woman in the world. Diana's joy in wearing good clothes is so apparent and her sense of fun in dressing up so innocent that everyone enjoys the show. Her vitality shines through and, even at her most svelte and sophisticated, the happy little girl in the toy shop can still be discerned.

Above: When glamour and elegance are called for, Diana can always rise to the occasion, but she never looks predictable. She quite clearly enjoys the fun of dressing up.

Right: Casual clothes for an informal occasion – Diana relaxes in comfortable clothes at Windsor. But, even in jeans and a T-shirt, she has eye-catching presence.

She has boldness in her approach and insists on doing what she thinks right for herself. Royal ladies have, understandably, always sacrificed fashion-consciousness for dignity, but Diana's self-assurance ensures that she will never lose her dignity if she follows her instincts. This allows her to take risks that no other royal lady would ever dare.

Balancing this boldness is an equally valuable sensitivity to the occasion and to her own role. Obviously, the kinds of clothes Diana wears for a great state occasion are very different from those she wears when visiting her local school at Tetbury. Both demand due judgement, but Diana takes this exercise into a new dimension. Any experienced lady-in-waiting can advise on what kinds of clothes to wear and when. Only Diana can decide the colour, the style, the designer, the fabric, and the accessories. Rightly, she trusts her own judgement.

She has scored a number of notable royal firsts too. Previously, it was unthinkable for a royal lady to buy clothes 'off-the-peg', but Diana has always enjoyed shopping in Knightsbridge and saw no reason to stop. Few journalists recognized the significance of the fact that, on her very first public encounter with the press, on the day of the official announcement of her engagement to Prince Charles, she was wearing a blue suit by Cojana bought 'off-the-peg' from Harrods. She has never been embarrassed about wearing ready-made clothes if she considers them suitable, and this is a sensible and shrewd decision in the light of the number of outfits she needs to carry out her public duties effectively.

She also buys her clothes from many different designers. In the past, royal ladies carefully chose their dress designers and the match was made for life. Both Norman Hartnell and Hardy Amies consolidated their reputations this way. Diana broke with tradition by deciding that no one designer, or even two or three, could possibly cope with the demands she was going to make. So she went 'shopping around' among designers, especially those who were young and unknown, to find the talent she wanted. No one can deny how splendidly she has succeeded.

Diana's tall, slim figure and strong sense of colour are complemented by her unerring instinct for the line and drape of her clothes, whether day or evening-wear. For example, when visiting the Sue Ryder Home in Gloucester (left), she wore a striking and practical blue woollen coat and matching off-the-face hat. For the Première of The Hunt for Red October, *she wore a shimmering jade evening dress, draped across the hips, and looked more glamorous even than a movie star (centre). For a banquet during the Gulf Tour (right), she wore a deceptively simple, formal gown in black and white duchesse satin, which featured a large, striped bow at the waist.*

ROYAL DESIGNERS

Diana has now made the reputation of a number of British dress designers. And she started as she intended to go on. There is no doubt that the most important clothes decision she would ever make would be the earliest – who would design and make her wedding dress. Even at the age of 20, she showed a sureness of touch by choosing two young designers, David and Elizabeth Emanuel. Although they were by no means unknown in the world of haute couture, it was still a bold and exciting choice. The Emanuels realized that this was to be a dream dress for a grand occasion in one of London's most dramatic settings – St Paul's Cathedral – and they designed a most glorious and dramatic wedding dress. It was made of silk taffeta in a delicate shade of ivory, with an overlay of lace encrusted with tiny pearls. The train was 25 feet long, and glistened with thousands of tiny pearls and mother-of-pearl sequins.

Not only her dress was a superb creation. Her wedding slippers too, were minor works of art created by Clive Shilton, the royal shoemaker. They were made of silk and were decorated with hearts made from 150 pearls and 500 sequins. The dress, shoes, and other accessories went on exhibition shortly after the wedding, and were admired by millions of people as they were shown all over the world. It was a fairytale dress for a fairytale occasion.

The list of designers used by Princess Diana is indeed formidable – so many, that it is easier to list them alphabetically rather than by date or function.

Murray Arbeid is a designer Princess Diana has commissioned for formal evening clothes.

Benetton is an Italian chain from whom Diana occasionally buys separates both for herself and the young Princes.

Alistair Blair, designer, is a Scot who took a first-class honours degree at the St Martin's School of Art. He went from there to become an assistant to Marc Bohan at the Christian Dior studio, followed by another two years at Givenchy. He then moved to Chloe to work under Karl Lagerfeld. He started his own couture business in 1985, and Princess Diana immediately recognized his talent the first time he showed. She is now a frequent client.

John Boyd is one of Diana's favourite milliners. She has worn his specially designed hats on many important occasions.

Lindka Cierach, designer, has an exotic background, from her birth in Lesotho in 1952 to her upbringing in Uganda. When she was eight years old she was sent to school in England. She left Britain for Paris where she spent nine months before returning to the family home in Cornwall. She got a job with *Vogue* magazine before becoming a star pupil at the London College of Fashion. Her first design job was with Yuki both in London and Paris before branching out on her own. She was discovered by the *Tatler* magazine and her first big success was the Duchess of York's wedding dress. Diana now buys from her too.

Chris Clyne has made some sporty dresses for Diana and she wore some of his clothes on her Australian tour in 1985.

Jasper Conran is another favoured designer. At the age of 16 he won a place at the famous fashion design college, Parsons' of New York. He was there between 1975 and 1977 when he went to work first for Fiorucci and then Wallis. He put on his own first show in 1978 and was almost immediately established as one of Britain's most exciting new designers. Princess Diana has several of his simple but brilliant outfits in her wardrobe.

Diana has become a world fashion-leader and should be given credit for the major role she has played in the renaissance of the British fashion industry. Unlike many other royal ladies, she does not restrict her choice to the creations of a single designer, but buys from an eclectic mix of both up-coming and established fashion houses. Hats are usually worn off the brow to avoid the risk of their blowing away and to allow people to see her face. She is especially fond of John Boyd's rather unusual, 18th-century style feathered hats (right). He also designed the hat for her going-away outfit. Her yellow and black hat (below) was designed by Philip Somerville specially for Diana's German tour. Diana's hairdresser is an essential contributor to her overall look. She changes the style of her hair quite frequently and sets trends in salons across the country and even abroad. In late 1984, for example, she chose a rather 1940s look (right).

Sometimes Diana breaks the 'rules', as with this delightful, shady, broad-brimmed hat worn during her tour of Australia in 1988 (left). She has an instinctive understanding of both colour and style and knows exactly what suits her. During the planning stage of any foreign tour, she works closely with designers, discussing the special requirements of climate, protocol and formal occasions. She has an artist's eye for the focal feature – a bow at the waist, an unusual collar, frogging, decorative buttons, or draped pleats. The dramatic red and black cocktail dress, with its eye-catching low back (left) that she wore to the première of Private Lives is typical of her flamboyant style. Similarly, Diana recognizes how well her colouring suits graphic patterns. She often chooses bold and sometimes unusual combinations of colours, in checks, spots and separates. This silk suit by Roland Klein (below) was designed for her Australian tour and she has also worn it at Ascot.

Paul Costelloe designed and made clothes for Diana's Australian tour.

Victor Edelstein trained with a number of star couture houses and worked with Jorn Langbom at Christian Dior from 1976 until 1978. He set up his own studio in Covent Garden, specializing in ready-to-wear clothes, but he soon returned to haute couture. His first commission from Diana was a pink taffeta maternity evening dress. Since then she has been a regular client.

David and Elizabeth Emanuel found immediate and lasting fame when they designed Diana's wedding dress. They were married in 1975 after meeting as students at the Harrow School of Art. They then went on to the Royal College of Art as that institution's first ever married couple. Their combined final presentation, all in white, was a triumph and the intense interest displayed by some of the smartest shops in London inspired them to go it alone. Their first collection in September 1977 was a sensation and they soon had many prestigious clients. They remain among Diana's favourite designers.

Escada is a German fashion house from whom Diana buys some of her casual co-ordinates.

Freddie Fox, one of Britain's most adventurous milliners, has made hats for special occasions for Diana among many other famous clients.

Hachi, a Japanese designer, was responsible for a breathtaking sequined evening gown Diana has worn on several festive occasions.

Hacker has made some highly original clothes for the Princess, including a famous green silk waistcoat.

Marina Killey is a milliner who has made some adventurous hats for the Princess among many other clients.

Roland Klein worked for Dior after leaving college in Paris. He then went on to work at Patou under Karl Lagerfeld. He came to London from Paris in 1965 and joined Marcel Fenez. He opened his own shop in Brook Street, Mayfair in 1979, and Diana much admires the wit and chic of his designs.

Viv Knowlands has designed some fetching hats for Diana, her most distinguished customer.

Ralph Lauren has made informal clothes for Diana, including delightful floral jeans.

Mondi, the famous German fashion house, have their own shop at Harrods. They have made skirts and sweaters for the Princess.

Christopher Morgan has worked alongside Bruce Oldfield in making original hats for Princess Diana.

Bruce Oldfield is perhaps the most interesting of Diana's favoured designers. He was fostered by a dressmaker and tailor, Miss Violet Masters, at the age of 18 months. After completing his education, he began a three-year teacher training course at Sheffield, before moving to London for a fashion and textile course at Ravensbourne College, changing to St Martin's School of Art. In 1972, he won the Saga Mink competition and soon commissions began to pour in. He held a solo show in New York, and in 1975 formed his own company in London. He soon found himself so overworked that he decided to concentrate on the top quality end of the market. Not surprisingly, his international clientele includes Diana.

Rifat Ozbek has recently been commissioned by Princess Diana.

Arabella Pollen had Diana as her most distinguished client. She started working for private clients in 1981 and in 1984 was commissioned to design the uniforms for *Virgin Atlantic Airlines*. She sells widely in the United States, Europe, and the Far East.

David Sassoon is another dress designer highly favoured by Diana in conjunction with his partner Belinda Belleville, whom he joined after leaving the Royal College of Art. They jointly formed Belleville Sassoon in 1953 and have never looked back. Not only do they number Diana among their clientele, but also Princess Margaret and the Duchesses of York and Kent. David Sassoon made many of Diana's engagement clothes and her going-away outfit, plus a complete maternity wardrobe for her first pregnancy.

Graham Smith is a milliner, who studied first at the Bromley College of Art and later at the Royal College of Art. He worked for a year with Lanvin in Paris, returning to London to work for Michael making hats. He soon began to work for himself and after 14 years, became Director of Design at Kangol. His extensive private clientele includes not only Princess Diana, but the Duchess of York and other distinguished ladies. Two of his designs are included in the fashion collection of the Victoria and Albert Museum.

Philip Somerville worked for the great milliner Otto Lucas for some years, but eventually began to work for himself. Diana much admires his work, as do the Duchesses of York and Kent and former Prime Minister Margaret Thatcher.

Jan Van Velden attended fashion college in Amsterdam before moving to London, where he also studied at the London College of Fashion. Princess Diana first commissioned him for an outfit for her royal tour of Australia in 1983. The Duchess of Kent and Princess Michael are also among his clients.

Catherine Walker has had Diana as one of her most faithful clients for over a decade. She designed one of the Princess's earliest maternity outfits, and went on to design dresses for many of her most important outings. She comes closest to being Diana's personal couturier in the traditional manner.

Kirsten Woodward is another milliner favoured by Diana.

This list is both impressive and incomplete. Princess Diana, both by inclination and a strong sense of public duty, is the most prestigious showcase for the work of Britain's designers and textile industry. However, she is not afraid to use foreign designers if she likes their work, although, of course, she only uses them for her informal clothes.

Here an important note needs to be made. London has not replaced Paris as the world's capital of fashion, but it is a very close second city. Yet a generation ago, although the collections of designers such as Norman Hartnell and Hardy Amies were well attended, the clientele and fashion writers present were almost entirely British. The London collections seldom made the front pages of the French or American editions of *Vogue*. Although it would be inaccurate to say that Princess Diana effected this transformation all by herself, no one could deny that she has been the single most powerful force in attracting the world's smartest and wealthiest women to the salons of London. From the time the first pictures of her in her famous black ball gown appeared in the smart magazines, fashion editors have kept a close watch on her. There is no question at all that Diana has made the international reputation of British designers and milliners, and the British fashion scene is now taken very seriously all over the world.

Diana's dress-sense is a national asset and her expenditure on clothes should be seen as a profitable national investment. It has been calculated that the British fashion industry, with all its ramifications, turns over up to £50 billion a year and makes an enormous contribution to Britain's balance of payments. Although Diana's part in this is not quantifiable, it is obviously not negligible. Thankfully, it is not likely that her valuable interest in clothes will diminish when she becomes Queen.

ADVISERS AND EXPERTS

Although Diana's fabled dress-sense seems to have developed with startling speed, it did, in fact, have some assistance. When circumstances demanded that she change from a private to a public figure, she had the good sense to consult the leading experts in the field – the editor and staff of *Vogue*. Anne Harvey and her colleagues on the magazine know all there is to know about the fashion scene, and were naturally anxious and willing to pass on their knowledge to the young Princess. She very quickly assimilated all the information she needed for her career as one of the world's best-dressed women.

She quickly became aware that she was in a uniquely influential position to promote British fashion and design both at home, and more importantly, abroad. She moved quickly and effectively. She broadened the traditional manner in which the Palace dealt with clothes, by involving the editor and staff of *Vogue* even more deeply. Now she was able to have the British collections properly and professionally vetted, and to introduce the practice of 'racking', whereby a rack of clothes is selected for her inspection by a fashion consultant to cover all the eventualities in her forthcoming public appearances. This practice put Diana quickly and firmly both on top and ahead of the fashion trends of the time, a position she has effortlessly maintained ever since.

Quite apart from these lessons, there were others that all royal ladies needed to absorb, and rules that all royal couturiers need to observe. No evening dress or formal gown can be made, however fine or delicate the material, without incorporating a small strengthened panel just across the breast. This is so that the bodice will not sag beneath the weight of any medals or official brooches that might have to be worn. Skirts should not be made too tight, in case Diana has to crouch down to talk to a child or someone lying ill in bed. Hat brims must not be so large that they make it difficult to get in and out of cars, obscure her face or could be blown off in a sudden gust of wind. They can also unintentionally overshadow shorter dignitaries that she might meet. So, although Diana has the height to carry them off well, she rarely wears broad-brimmed hats.

Her clothes must not be garish, but should be bright enough to identify her easily in a crowd. This is also why Diana rarely wears simple black and white outfits during the day. She must also be aware of the vagaries of the weather: a dress in an unsuitable fabric might cling embarrassingly to her in a sudden downpour.

As it is sensible to wear very expensive dresses more than once, a special 'log' is kept to make sure they are not worn twice at the same kind of function or in the same part of the country. Diana also has her own unique way of 'filing' her clothes. As Lesley Ebbetts says:

With the help of her dresser, Evelyn Dagley, the Princess has a system within her large dressing room, off the enormous main bedroom in Kensington Palace. Everything there is arranged according to colour, hanging in its own protective cover. Even the accessories, shoes and belts are kept in their own cupboards and stored by colour.

In 1986, when Diana's long-standing friend, Sarah Ferguson, married Prince Andrew, the press was unable to resist the temptation of making comparisons between these two young royals. It was suggested that Diana and Sarah were somehow in competition and a fallacious style war hit the headlines. In fact, the Duchess of York has established her own distinctive style, matched to her more exuberant personality and less demanding lifestyle.

Planting a tree in the pouring rain is hardly the ideal condition for a display of elegance, but Diana remained unruffled as bystanders shielded her with umbrellas.

FINISHING TOUCHES

Although dressing-up for Britain is an essentially serious business, this does not mean to say that Diana and her designers – and the clothes they make for her – can never be light-hearted. Diana is quite fond of visual jokes like *trompe l'oeil* sweaters, flower-power jeans, and necklaces converted to jewelled headbands. On her Italian tour, Jasper Conran included a black bow tie on one of his outfits, a joke that everyone enjoyed.

Diana likes her clothes to be fun and she often incorporates entertaining features or even a completely unconventional outfit, if the occasion allows. She set a new trend in women's fashions when she wore a white tuxedo and black bow tie at the Exhibition Centre in Solihull in 1984.

Foreign tours, though, have to be taken seriously and involve a lot of careful pre-planning. There are endless discussions about what outfits would best suit each public appearance, what kind of fabrics are most appropriate for the climate and, generally, how Great Britain can best be presented and promoted throughout the trip. Diana also likes subtly to flatter the national feelings of her hosts: she wore a dress patterned with red rising suns for a visit to Japan and a dress using the colours of the national flag on a visit to Germany. Her hosts were touched by this thoughtful attention to detail. She also likes to pay graceful compliments to the women of her host countries, such as when she wore a hat shaped like a mantilla on her visit to Spain.

When it comes to her personal jewellery, Diana prefers simplicity to ornate display. She dislikes brooches and only wears them when she has to; for example, she wears the official badge of a regiment of which she is Colonel-in-Chief. She does like pearls and wears them whenever she can.

Her hairdresser, Richard Dalton, plays an important part in her public life and she has complete confidence in his advice and his handiwork. He gave up his key post at Headliners in London to concentrate on Diana's hair and it is due to his supreme expertise that she can be seen with as many different hairstyles as there are occasions when she needs them. He was preceded by his old employer, Kevin Shanley, whose family circumstances prevented him from giving Diana the constant night and day attention that she needs. Proof of Richard Dalton's sure touch is that Diana's hairstyles are quickly imitated in hairdressing salons the length of the country – and widely abroad too.

CHAPTER 5

WIFE
AND
MOTHER

The wedding and honeymoon over, it was time for reality. As third lady in the land, the Princess has set her own style, gradually adapting to the established routine of the Royal Family, yet incorporating her own ideas.

Like any young married couple, Charles and Diana needed a new home, but as Prince and Princess of Wales, they required two residences. First, they needed a permanent residence in London. Although there is plenty of room at Buckingham Palace, protocol demands that they have a residence of their own, with their own possessions and permanently staffed secretarial offices. (There are always apartments at Buckingham Palace available for their use on special occasions, but these are few and far between.) The most obviously suitable home for the heir to the throne would have been Clarence House just off the Mall and within five-minutes walking distance from Buckingham Palace. However, this is still the official residence of the Queen Mother and, although time will one day make Clarence House available to them, at the time of Charles's marriage in 1981 it was not an option.

Apartments in West London's Kensington Palace, which has been owned by the Crown since 1689, were chosen as the most suitable residence for the newlyweds. The Palace is already the London home of Princess Margaret, Prince and Princess Michael of Kent, and the Duke and Duchess of Gloucester.

During its long history, Kensington Palace has known many changes. Even its name was changed to Nottingham House when it was owned by the Earl of Nottingham. It reverted to Kensington Palace when William III and Mary purchased the house. Sir Christopher Wren designed extensive alterations to adhere to a traditional pattern of royal homes, with the King's apartments on the right and the Queen's on the left. During restoration work following a serious fire in 1691, the great architect completed the King's Gallery. Over the centuries it has been the home of many kings and queens. Thirteen of King George III's children grew up there; Queen Victoria was born and christened there, and it was also the birthplace of Queen Mary, wife of George V.

Three floors at 8-9 Kensington Palace were converted for the use of the Prince and Princess of Wales. The apartment was extensively redecorated by the designer Dudley Poplak, and there is a private roof garden with its own greenhouse and barbecue, ideal for secluded sunbathing or summer outdoor parties. It remains their official London residence.

Below: Charles and Diana spent their honeymoon cruising in the Mediterranean on the royal yacht Britannia and also visited President Sadat of Egypt. When they flew home to Britain, they spent a little time at Balmoral before embarking on a new round of public duties.

Previous page: Proud and delighted parents, the Prince and Princess of Wales left St Mary's Hospital with their newborn son, William, swathed in a shawl.

HIGHGROVE

During 1980 Prince Charles decided that it was time he had a family home in the country for himself and – unspokenly – for his future wife. He presented a formidable list of requirements to the firm of Smith-Wooley of Woodstock, who began the search. The house had to be in the real country, not in a rural suburb, but within easy reach of London. It had to have a home farm. It had to be all of a piece, so that he could build a wall round it, he needed somewhere where he could be absolutely sure of complete privacy so that he could give himself and his future family some kind of normal private life.

At the end of a long search only one house fulfilled all these requirements – Highgrove near Tetbury, in Gloucestershire. The mansion was built in the 18th century, and was set in some 350 acres of fields and secluded woods. It had other advantages, too. It is near the M4 and thus easily accessible from London, has a home farm, and it could be easily walled. Another very important asset is that there is plenty of space for the royal helicopter to land.

Highgrove was owned by Maurice Macmillan, a Conservative Member of Parliament and son of the former Prime Minister. Charles paid over £750,000 for it and moved in as soon as he could. He kept on the services of Mr and Mrs Whiteland who had acted as cook-housekeeper and general factotum to Maurice Macmillan, and this proved a wise as well as a kind decision. They knew the house and its surroundings intimately and were able to protect him and, later, his new wife and family from many worries and intrusions.

He felt completely relaxed at Highgrove and stayed there as long and as often as he could. Already a keen gardener, Prince Charles made many changes, including a walled garden complete with minaret arch inspired by the Taj Mahal. A wildflower garden was another lovely innovation.

The newlyweds moved in during the late summer of 1981, preceded by several pantechnicons full of wedding presents. The house had been lovingly prepared for its new occupants and, after the pomp of the wedding and the publicity surrounding the honeymoon, the peace and quiet of the Gloucestershire countryside must have been wonderfully relaxing. Alas, it was not to last for long and all too soon Charles and his new Princess had to return to London to take up the heavy round of public engagements expected of all royal persons.

Highgrove offered many advantages as a family home for the Prince and Princess of Wales. Many friends and other members of the Royal Family live nearby, including Princess Anne, whose country home is at Gatcombe Park, and Prince and Princess Michael of Kent. It is only a short drive from Windsor, and not too far from the principality of Wales nor from the Prince's estates in the Duchy of Cornwall. It is close to a number of racecourses (Newbury, Cheltenham, Chepstow, and Bath), and there is polo nearby at Cowdray Park and Smith's Lawn.

PUBLIC ENGAGEMENTS

By now, Diana had her own staff, including one full-time Lady-in-Waiting, Anne Beckwith-Smith, and two part-timers, Hazel West and Lavinia Baring. These ladies play an important role in the royal life, and need stamina, a sense of humour and the ability to act quickly in an emergency. They carry the 'disaster kit' in case tights are torn, gloves are dropped, or a hemline needs a pin.

To begin with, Diana shared most of her important engagements with her husband, but soon she began to undertake some on her own. In a remarkably

Diana's first public function as Princess of Wales was a tour of the principality. Many adults and thousands of children waited long hours in cold weather to see her, and she did not disappoint them. She mingled with people, chatting and shaking hands on a royal 'walkabout'.

short space of time she settled into a punishing routine. Like most of the Royal Family, she is inundated with requests for visits from towns and organizations, but these have to be planned months in advance. The Lady-in-Waiting and other staff, including Security, need to go on a reconnaissance of any intended visit, noting the names (and history) of those to be presented, anything outstanding about the town or building, and any special circumstance likely to cause embarrassment for a woman, such as descending a ladder aboard ship. Every detail is carefully noted and the Princess is extensively briefed in advance to ensure the smooth running of the operation. Streets are specially cleaned and barriers erected to contain the crowd. Red carpets are often laid for her to walk on, roads are closed and parking is restricted where it would impede the royal cars. A royal visitor must never arrive too early – or very late.

The Lady-in-Waiting also acts as a secretary, although the thousands of letters sent to the Palace from all over the world are centrally sorted.

Two of the most important people on the Princess's staff are her dressers. They are responsible for all her clothes, all of which are listed, with a note of the occasions on which they have been worn and with what accessories. The garments are very carefully maintained and cared for. As the Princess likes to add variety to her clothes, often by mixing items from different outfits, the records have to be very accurate and up to date.

It is more than 70 years since there was last a Princess of Wales (Mary, later to become Queen Mary) so, as the world has changed, so have many of the old ideas and customs surrounding the Royal Family. Debutantes are no longer presented at court, as in the past, but regular garden parties are held. Perhaps the biggest change of all is the royal 'walkabout', which affords greater accessibility to the public at large.

Princess Diana's first public function was, appropriately enough, a ceremonial visit to Wales. It was her first exposure as Princess of Wales to a really large crowd, and she carried it off superbly. It was October and people waited at the roadside in chilling winds to get a glimpse of her as she was driven past. Often the car went slowly enough for people to reach out and touch their beautiful new Princess. The couple covered 400 miles in three days and visited every kind of place: holiday resorts, factories, historic buildings, mines, and hospitals. Caernarvon, where the Prince's investiture in 1969 had taken place was naturally on the itinerary. Charles was able to show his wife the place where he had sworn allegiance, and then, symbolically, presented her to the people from the Queen's Gate to resounding cheers. Cardiff was the finale, where the Princess became the fifty-third Freeman of the City, only the second woman to be so honoured. She was presented with a silver casket containing the Freedom Scroll and made a short speech of thanks, even managing a few words in Welsh to the delight of all.

Diana met hundreds of people, and everywhere she went there were crowds, crowds, crowds. They were expecting a fairytale princess – and they got one. From the beginning Diana was to demonstrate her stunning dress sense, her exact understanding of when to startle and when to be demure. It was on this Welsh visit that she first 'went walkabout' and, daringly, ventured into the crowd to talk directly to her husband's people. It was a triumph; especially for so inexperienced a public figure. It was also a valuable lesson in how to deal with people directly. These same people were her husband's future subjects and, as his Queen, she would need to know how to project that precise combination of friendliness and distance which is the hallmark of the British monarchy.

Charles and Diana visited Caernarvon Castle and the Prince showed his wife the scene of his formal investiture. He then presented her to the Welsh people at the Queen's Gate.

Left: Attending film premières is one of the less onerous tasks that Diana has to undertake – but, in any case, she quickly learned to conceal any feelings of boredom or lack of interest.

The Queen has always recognized that the formality of her grandfather's court was unacceptably remote in modern times and so she was quite prepared to be photographed in gum boots in the stables at Sandringham or wearing a headscarf on an informal ride. But she also knew that a certain mystique was equally essential; the British people like their Queen to be truly royal. Her new daughter-in-law would have to learn the same lesson if she was to be a successful Queen. In Wales she showed that she was beginning to learn the necessary lessons.

At the beginning of November, the Prince and Princess of Wales opened the 25th London Film Festival at the South Bank's National Film Theatre. Again, Diana's dress was a sensation and, not for the last time, all eyes were on her rather than on her husband. This focus of general and, especially, media attention on her was to persist and grow. Far from being resentful, Prince Charles warmly welcomed this phenomenon.

November 4 saw one of the great days of the royal calendar – the State Opening of Parliament by the Queen. Although during her engagement and first weeks of married life Diana had shown herself to be an instinctively elegant dresser, the State Opening was an occasion for really dressing up. Although it is not possible (nor sensible) to upstage the Queen, it was Diana's dress that everyone wanted to see. She rose to the occasion in resplendent white dress and tiara. The impact was only increased by the fact that she was the first Princess of Wales to attend the State Opening of Parliament for 70 years. The same evening she helped the Prince of Wales inaugurate the 'Splendours of the Gonzaga' at the Victoria and Albert Museum, of which Prince Charles is a patron.

The next day, came the news that the Royal Family, the British people, and, in fact, the whole world was waiting for. It was in the form of a simple statement from Buckingham Palace: 'The Princess of Wales is expecting a baby next June. The Prince and Princess of Wales, the Queen and the Duke of Edinburgh, and members of both families are delighted by the news.' This statement also followed. 'The Princess is in excellent health. She hopes to undertake some public engagements but regrets the disappointment that may be caused by any curtailment in her planned programme.'

When Diana became pregnant soon after her marriage, she had to cancel a few public engagements because she felt unwell, but whenever possible she endeavoured to avoid disappointing people.

In effect, this meant that Diana's projected tour of Australia in 1982 had to be cancelled or temporarily postponed. She had been looking forward to this very much, not least because her step-father, Peter Shand-Kydd, owned a sheep-farm there and this would have offered the chance for some relief from the endless round of public engagements she and her husband would be expected to undertake. As it turned out, the promised visit took place in March 1983 and lasted for six weeks. The Prince kept the promise made on his Australian tour the previous year that he would return bringing his wife. In fact, he brought not only his wife, but his son, Prince William. The visit was an outstanding success and the Australians showed their appreciation. One touching moment was the symbolic visit of the Prince and Princess to Ayer's Rock, a place held sacred by the aborigines.

There was no reason for a healthy young woman in the early stages of pregnancy to curtail any of her immediate public engagements, and Diana made the point very simply herself by fulfilling a lunch engagement with the Lord Mayor of London and 600 distinguished guests at the Guildhall in the City of London just two hours after the public announcement of her pregnancy. Word had not yet travelled very far, and the Lord Mayor was able to break the news to the delighted company.

The week ended with her attendance, together with other members of the

Pregnancy prevented Diana undertaking the tour of Australia planned for 1982. While this was immediately disappointing, the Australian people were more than compensated the following year by a visit from not only the Prince and Princess of Wales, but from baby William, too.

Royal Family, at the annual Royal British Legion Festival of Remembrance at the Albert Hall. Next morning the Princess watched from a balcony in Whitehall as the Queen, Prince Philip, and others laid wreaths at the Cenotaph.

During the next few weeks, Diana had to cancel a number of engagements, as she was 'unwell'. It does not need a very educated guess to infer that morning sickness finds victims at every level of society. But, apart from these few disappointments, she continued to be assiduous in fulfilling her royal ration of public obligations. Her next appearance was with Prince Charles at York, where they visited the railway museum and went on an informal walkabout in the city centre. Later, thousands of children cheered the couple in the city stadium before the Prince took her off in the royal helicopter to Chesterfield to open a shopping precinct and a police headquarters.

In November, she undertook her first solo engagement. It was simple enough: switching on the Christmas lights in London's Regent Street. Nevertheless, it was still a daunting experience for a young woman whose public appearances had previously been with the presence, support, and encouragement of her husband. In the past, she had always had the reassurance that if the slightest thing went wrong, Charles was there to sort it all out. From now she could and would be on her own. The simple pressing of a Christmas switch signalled another stage in her royal progress.

The end of 1981 saw a flurry of activity for Princess Di, as she was increasingly called. She was simultaneously trying to settle down with her still new husband at their home at Highgrove, adjusting to the idea of impending motherhood, and carrying out a taxing programme of public engagements. The public-private dichotomy of royal life was inexorably imposing itself upon her life.

On 20 November, she planted her first tree in Hyde Park. She was given a helping hand by her smiling husband, but it was the precursor of many other tree plantings she would have to perform alone. This unique symbol of royal interest and approval seems simple enough in principle, but, again, it has to be carefully prepared for and rehearsed. Muddy royal shoes cannot be allowed to spoil the next appointment, so no high heels or elegant court shoes can be worn. Practicality demands flat and sensible footwear. Details like this must be considered for every public appearance. The first planting was truly a baptism of fire because there was not one, but three cherry trees for her to plant, with three more for Charles.

Diana's next solo appearance followed shortly afterwards when she opened the new Head Post Office at Northampton. This was farther from home than Regent Street and more demanding than pressing a switch, but she played her role more than adequately and demonstrated a warm informality which was to become one of the recognized pleasures of a visit from the Princess. She operated some complicated machinery under the watchful eyes of the photographers, and this second personal appearance on her own was judged a great success.

Another piece of the royal jigsaw was now set in place. This was to learn to sit through long concerts, operas, ballets, plays, command performances, and so on without falling asleep or, indeed, showing the slightest sign of inattention. It would not be humanly possible for any royal person, least of all a lively young woman, to enjoy every second of every artistic performance she attends. It is also no secret that, like most young people, the Princess prefers pop to Poulenc, although she is known to be fond of ballet. She dutifully attended three programmes – one ballet and two operas – at the Royal Opera House Covent Garden. She behaved with grace and charm.

Diana enjoys meeting people and mixing with the crowds. The informal style that has characterized the Royal Family's visits in recent years, including the famous 'walkabouts', exactly matches her own inclinations. Even the police and other security staff enjoy these occasions, in spite of the extra anxiety they must inevitably cause.

On 26 November, the new Princess safely overcame yet another hurdle on the long road to queenship – a gathering of heavyweight world statesmen. All the heads of the member governments of the European Economic Community visited London for an important conference and were invited to lunch with the Queen at Buckingham Palace. The Prince and Princess of Wales were included among the guests. For any 20-year-old, this gathering of august prime ministers would have been a daunting experience. For Diana, who was undoubtedly under discreet scrutiny as the future Queen of the United Kingdom, it must have been exceptionally heavy going, even with the support of her husband. Meeting and

In some ways, Diana is like a breath of fresh air to the Royal Family. A young, lively woman, she clearly enjoys some of her more lighthearted duties, especially those which capture her particular interest. Here she is seen chatting to Duran Duran at a Charity Gala Concert in London.

making small talk – and sometimes not very small talk – with foreign statesmen and stateswomen is part of the required equipment of a queen. Again, Diana was learning the lessons she needed to guide her smoothly and efficiently towards the consort's throne.

At the other end of the scale was Princess Diana's role at the local level. Highgrove's neighbouring village of Tetbury took a highly proprietorial view of 'their' royals and guarded their privacy jealously. They invited the Prince and Princess to participate in as many local activities as they could manage. When the royal engagement had been announced in February, the children of St Mary's school at Tetbury had written a letter of congratulations, and she had given it the best possible reply by promising to visit them as soon as she possibly could. She fulfilled this promise early in December, driving herself from Highgrove in her own silver Ford Escort, joining in the carols, attending morning assembly and visiting every classroom in the school. She admired the model nativity the children had made and finally presented the school with a paperweight engraved with Prince-of-Wales feathers. She continues to take an interest in this local school and its activities. In spite of all the difficulties she encounters, she still uses the local shops for casual purchases and joins in as many local activities as she can. She does her best, in fact, to be a good neighbour. This care for and interest in the people she lives among is a microcosm of her future role as a good neighbour to the whole of the British people.

The Princess was, naturally, in great demand. Few people can remember a time when there was a Princess of Wales, so everyone wanted her to visit *them*, and enthusiasm for her was running high. As Princesses of Wales were traditionally noted (as are other members of the Royal Family) for their good works, many organizations and societies sought her patronage. From the outset, the Princess was determined to give her patronage only to those organizations in which she was particularly interested and could play an active role. She had no intention of merely being a name on writing paper.

Children, of course, and youth groups, were high on the list. The arts – music and ballet – cancer research, the deaf (she learned sign language to be able to communicate with them), and the disabled all drew her personal attention. At a meeting with many disabled people in the gardens of Buckingham Palace to present specially adapted vehicles, she smilingly waved the keys and asked, with her inborn spontaneity, who was going to *clean* the car?

Many medical causes were to feature on her list: cancer, children's illnesses, drug and alcohol abuse, mental problems, smoking and health, spinal research, Parkinson's disease and leprosy. All were to occupy much of her time and to gain her sympathy and understanding. Wildlife and sport were not to be forgotten. The Princess was to honour Gloucestershire Cricket Club, and even attended an annual dinner!

Her patronage was not confined to Britain, and causes in the Commonwealth were also to feature in her efforts.

There were still a few official functions before she would be allowed a few days' holiday at Christmas. There was a ceremonial visit to the local cathedral at Gloucester to celebrate its 1300th anniversary, and a week later a visit to another cathedral; this time the modern cathedral at Guildford for a Christmas celebration in support of the Prince's Trust. In spite of the bitter December cold, Diana and Charles chose to go 'walkabout' after the service. The next day they were in London again for a visit to the Manor of Kensington, this time in their role as Duke and Duchess of Cornwall.

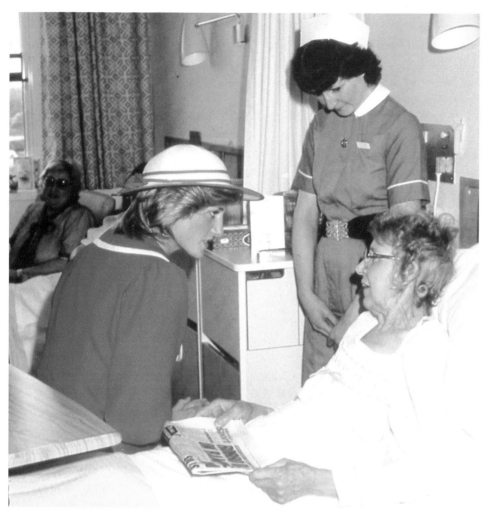

Diana's warmth and sympathy towards those ill, frail or suffering in some way is spontaneous and genuine. Her sincerity is apparent to anyone who has witnessed her visits to hospitals or children's homes. She has always had an instinctive rapport with children and a readiness to pay proper attention to their concerns. On a visit to the Palladium in London's West End (above), Diana was captured in earnest conversation with a young, disabled fan. It is quite obvious that Diana's visit to Preston Hospital in 1983 (left above) proved to be a tonic to the elderly patient to whom she is listening with genuine concern. Children's charities are very special to Diana, and she is no mere figurehead. She likes to be kept informed of their activities and to visit as frequently as possible. When she visited Tunbridge Wells (left), Diana really got down to serious telephone talk!

Never one to stand on ceremony, with hardly a thought for her dignity or comfort, Diana dropped easily to her knees to talk more intimately to one of the blind people she was visiting in 1982 (right). A keen swimmer herself, she reclined on the poolside in Ipswich (below) to talk to the children in the water.

FAMILY LIFE

Princess Diana's first royal year ended traditionally with the Royal Family gathered at Windsor. Although these are essentially private, family occasions, they follow in essence the practice laid down by Queen Victoria and Prince Albert almost a century and a half ago. The new Princess was initiated into the Royal Christmas, with all its idiosyncracies, its cheerful and solemn moments, and its own particular celebrations. This first Christmas was also the first time she experienced the Royal Family *en masse*.

Apart from the Queen and the Duke of Edinburgh, those present included Princess Alice, Dowager Duchess of Gloucester who, incidentally, reached her eightieth birthday on Christmas Day. By coincidence, Christmas Day is also the birthday of Princess Alexandra. It was her forty-fifth birthday, and she was there with her husband, the Hon. Angus Ogilvy. The Queen Mother, Princess Margaret, and the Princes Edward and Andrew, the Duke and Duchess of Kent and their children, the Duke and Duchess of Gloucester, their children, and Princess Anne and her husband Mark Phillips were all at Windsor for the Christmas celebrations.

Three days after Christmas, the party broke up and the families went their various ways. As an immediate member of the Royal Family, Princess Diana accompanied her husband to Sandringham, where they joined the Queen, the Duke of Edinburgh, Prince Andrew, Prince Edward, and the Queen Mother. For Diana, Sandringham had been the house next door in her childhood days and, in some ways, it must have been like going home. After the holiday it was back to Highgrove to await the arrival of her first baby, due in the second half of June.

Diana has always shown a warmth towards and an affinity with children, so the birth of Prince William early in her marriage was undoubtedly a special joy. Both the Prince and Princess of Wales have made every attempt to give their sons as normal a family life as possible. Coming late to fatherhood, Charles has shown himself to be a surprisingly modern and sensitive parent, while Diana takes obvious pride and pleasure in motherhood. Here they can be seen playing with the baby Prince at Kensington Palace.

As well as her visible public role as the Princess of Wales and representative of the Royal Family, Diana has another and perhaps even more important role – Charles's wife. Although her vivacity and beauty often eclipse his own more sober qualities, no one should forget that his position determines hers. He is the future King and Head of State. It is his head that will appear on the coinage and stamps. He will be in the history books, and the laws of the land will be ratified under his seal. Diana will be his consort, but when he dies, his eldest son will succeed. However important it is, hers is and constitutionally must be a subordinate role.

Thus she has another key role – wife to the Prince and mother of his children. Perhaps her most important job is to offer the support, encouragement and comfort he needs to do his job effectively. This cannot be an easy part to play. At one moment, she is ceremonially robed and perfectly turned out at his side on some public occasion where almost every word and movement are as pre-determined as a stage play. The next she is with him behind closed doors where as his closest companion she can care for him as only a woman can, sympathizing, soothing, giving him strength and reassurance.

Charles is a sensitive man, in some ways ill-suited to the continuous and back-breaking slog of royal public life. He is clearly sometimes hurt by public criticism, however ill-informed or spiteful. So Diana has a wifely role in seeing that he does not take life too seriously and that, safe behind the walls of Highgrove, he can indulge himself as a farmer, a gardener, a designer or whatever relaxes him. As a young married couple they have shared all the normal delights of setting up home, placing the furniture, and discussing ways of using their wedding presents. Like any couple, they must have had many friendly arguments about the details of their domestic arrangements.

Son of the Heir Apparent and in direct line of succession to the throne, Prince William learned early to face the barrage of press and photographers eager to record his every move. With a charming lack of self-consciousness, he faces the news team in the grounds of Kensington Palace on the occasion of his second birthday.

MOTHERHOOD

The first day at school is exciting but a bit nerve-racking – even for a Prince. The comforting hand of a loving mother and the supportive presence of a caring father help a boy preserve his public composure.

Although Charles had no choice but to continue his punishing round of official duties, Diana's advancing pregnancy meant that she was relieved of all these and spent most of her time in tranquillity at Highgrove. Nevertheless she was with her husband as often as possible, and he was obviously pleased and proud of her as any other husband at such a time.

The baby was due in the second half of June and when Diana went into the first stages of labour early on 21 June, Charles took her to St Mary's Hospital in Paddington. They had moved to London to be ready for the birth. There is a private wing at St Mary's, called the Lindo Wing, where royal babies are born these days. Mr George Pinker, the Queen's obstetrician who had attended Diana throughout her pregnancy, was at hand.

Prince William was born at 9 pm on 21 June, just 10 days before Diana's twenty-first birthday. A healthy baby, he weighed just over 3 kg (7 lb). Charles was present throughout and had the joyful experience of seeing his son come into the world. As a father, he must have been glad that the baby had arrived without complications. As Prince of Wales, he must also have been pleased that the child was a boy; the succession had been ensured.

At 10 pm, the news was announced to a waiting world. An hour later, a tired but triumphant Charles emerged from the Lindo Wing to be greeted by the inevitable crowd of reporters and photographers. He bandied a few cheerful words with them and hurried off. He was back the next morning to take his wife and new son home, and was photographed with them, his son wrapped in a white shawl.

The next week, the Very Important Baby was named William Arthur Philip Louis. This last name was in honour of Earl Mountbatten, who had been both Prince Charles's and the Duke of Edinburgh's chief friend and adviser before his assassination. The names of the godparents were also announced: Natalia, the Duchess of Westminster, Lady Susan Hussey, Sir Laurens van der Post, a much admired older friend of the Prince, and three relatives, King Constantine, the former King of Greece, Princess Alexandra, and Lord Romsey.

Both Diana and Charles were determined to give their son as normal a childhood as possible. Sadly, this is something of a forlorn hope. Royal children stand little chance of living like ordinary children: the life their parents have to live effectively prevents it. No young Prince can have that day in, day out contact with his parents, especially with his mother, that ordinary boys and girls take for granted. For most children, a grazed knee, a bumped arm, an unexpected fall will summon Mummy, with kisses, cuddles and soothing words. For a royal child, all too often, Mummy will be 100 or 1000 miles away. For all their privilege and luxury, royal children have to pay a heavy price for their birthright.

In June 1983, the Prince and Princess made a 17-day trip to Canada. Once again the crowds clamoured for Diana, enthralled by her charm and spontaneity. Especially popular was an outfit of the 'Klondike era' with bustle and train which she wore for a music hall-style entertainment in which everyone joined.

In February 1984, on her return from a solo visit to Norway, it was announced that the Princess of Wales was expecting a second child in the autumn.

Charles and Diana's second child, also a son, was born on 18 September, 1984. He was christened Henry although he is universally known as Harry. A former flatmate and friend of the Princess, Mrs Carolyn Bartholomew, was one of his godmothers.

Whenever possible, Diana likes the children to travel with her, even when they were just babies. She and Harry are shown here clearly glad to be back home.

Diana's path to queenship is inevitably attended by the profound disadvantage of not being able to be with her children when she wants them or they want her. However, Diana and Charles, both together and separately, try to see their children for as long and as often as they can and to establish what can only be described as a caring routine whenever this is possible, especially at times like holidays from school. The family lives at Kensington Palace and the young Princes attend a London school. They always get away to Highgrove as often as they can to relax and enjoy family life.

Diana took instinctive delight in caring for her babies during their earliest years. She was little more than a girl when William was born and still a very young woman at Harry's birth, so she was young enough to enjoy them both to the full. As a royal mother, she has succeeded beyond all expectation, and the two boys appear to be healthy and happy youngsters who will be both physically and psychologically able to bear the burdens which will all too soon be laid upon them. Charles, too, has been a loving and caring father, much more so than anyone previously in his position has allowed himself to be.

Diana has matured and developed more than in years as a wife and mother. Although the first flush of young love and adoration of her husband has been replaced by a more mature affection and understanding of the need for mutual support, she is still very conscious of herself in her domestic role both in Kensington and in the more relaxed atmosphere of Highgrove. The 1990s will undoubtedly see her develop into a wise and mature woman.

Above: Charles and Diana try hard to find some private time with their family. A holiday in Majorca was the ideal opportunity to relax and enjoy the twin pleasures of sunshine and parenthood.

Right: Wills and Harry are now schoolboys and the family is based in Kensington Palace (the boys attend a London school). Nevertheless, they all escape to the privacy of Highgrove as often as their busy lives will permit.

CHAPTER 6
THE WORLD'S MOST PHOTOGRAPHED WOMAN

Whenever you see television footage of Princess Diana at some public function you will notice a curious and continuous flickering which could be mistaken for some malfunction of the television camera. This is by no means the case. The flickering is, in fact, the continual coruscation of a dozen... 50...100 flashguns, as eager photographers attempt to capture her every movement.

It has been this way since she burst upon the world as Prince Charles's girlfriend, with the serious possibility of becoming his bride. There was an immediate explosion of interest which has remained at a level approaching hysteria ever since. Wherever she goes in public, she is attended by a rat-pack of photographers, jostling for the best position.

Previous page: Diana is as popular a subject for amateur – or even junior – photographers as she is for professionals.

Below: Hygienically garbed for a visit to a marmalade factory, Diana is still as pretty as a picture.

ROYAL CHARISMA

What special quality does Diana have that can turn decent, hardworking photographers into hoodlums? Why do they wait for hours in freezing rain or the heat of midday, just for the chance – and it can never be a certainty – of a few hurried shots of a young woman coming out of a car and going into a door or coming out of a door and getting into a car? What makes Diana so special in the frenetic world of the photographer?

The first reason is the most obvious: Diana is highly photogenic. This is not the same thing as being beautiful, although Diana is beautiful, too. It is a curious

Any event in the lives of the Wales's is an instant signal for photographers to congregate in the hope of some interesting pictures.

fact that the very top fashion models have never been beautiful in the conventional sense. Twiggy, the star model of some 20 years ago, was extraordinarily skinny as her name implies, while Yasmin Le Bon is perhaps best described as eye-catching. This special 'on camera' quality seems to have something to do with bone structure, fluidity of movement, and the way clothes 'hang'.

Certainly Diana is photogenic, and she knows it. It means that she can get away with wearing casual clothes that would make other women look lumpy. But Diana is never 'casual' in the accepted sense. She knows exactly what effect she wants to achieve and seldom fails. Time and experience have given her the confidence to move with ease and assurance through any and every situation. The shy, gauche teenager whom Charles courted has long been superseded by the mature woman, and the young girl who blushed through her smiles when saucy photographers shouted personal remarks at her has long disappeared.

Another reason why Diana has remained photogenic for a decade is that, paradoxically, she has managed to retain an air of innocence in a situation where this ought to be impossible. She is now a mature woman, the mother of two sons, a Princess who has mixed on equal terms with many of the world's most learned, sophisticated, and powerful men and women. Yet she still manages to project an essential innocence, a wide-eyed wonder at the world and all its vagaries. This cannot be learned nor can it be turned on or off like a tap. It is an essential part of the character of Diana herself. To make an interesting comparison, it is a quality that Marilyn Monroe also possessed and accounts in part for her lasting quality. It is likely that Diana will retain this rare characteristic for as long as she lives.

Another aspect of Diana's appeal to photographers is that she has retained many of the qualities that endeared her so much to the hard-bitten lensmen who first besieged her flat and the Young England Kindergarten. Early photographs show Diana as a chubby and unexceptional baby and then as an attractive blonde toddler. She developed into a pretty child and one can detect in photographs of Diana the schoolgirl, the earliest signs of one of her most attractive attributes: the manner in which she bows her head and raises her eyes when she is surprised by photographers. It occurs only rarely these days, but does still happen. Psychologists say that it is a classic shyness response and there is a wealth of evidence that Diana was a shy little girl, but in an odd way, it has survived into adulthood. Diana can still look shy and vulnerable. In a world of hard-bitten and cynical public figures it is a priceless asset; the more so because it is patently not contrived or artificial. It is a kind of inner light that somehow she has managed to retain.

Diana also has another and more obvious quality: she was a genuinely lovely girl who has developed into a strikingly beautiful woman. She has all the qualities of a classic English beauty; she is tall, slim, blonde, and blue-eyed. But a list like this tells only half the story. She is certainly tall – tall enough to make her husband look quite short on occasions (one reason why she often wears flat-heeled shoes when they attend public occasions together). However, she is so well-proportioned that in photographs her height is not particularly noticeable. Photographs, of course, never lie, but they can give misleading impressions. Diana is so familiar to people through photographs that they are nearly always surprised at her height when they actually meet her.

Princess Diana is slim with excellent bone structure. Neither voluptuous nor skinny, she has an elegant, feminine figure.

Blonde she is, too, but this simple word savours too much of the tabloid press.

She always had glossy, golden hair. Early photographs show a child with a solemn little face framed by an sweep of light, straight tresses. She is fortunate in having luxuriant hair, which can be easily controlled and kept in place. From adolescence, Diana has taken particular care of her hair, and her hairdresser is on constant call to prepare her for every public appearance. Subtle changes are made to suit the occasion; a few simple modifications ensure that her hair is perfect and elegant for a state occasion or careless and casual for a local shopping expedition. Experienced photographers know that, contrary to appearance, the casual look is no less expertly achieved than the most formal. Where Diana leads, other women follow, and her hairstyles have been imitated by admiring women all over the world.

Are Diana's eyes really blue? Some people say they are, others claim that they are grey, yet others that they are hazel. Certainly they are not the clear blue that traditionally grace the features of the classical English rose. Perhaps the most interesting comment on Diana's eyes was made by an experienced model who said that Diana was lucky in that her eyes always harmonized with the clothes she was wearing at the time.

But still the sum of all these aspects of Diana's personality does not totally explain the fascination she has for photographers and for the editors of the world's magazines and newspapers. Her face on the cover of a woman's magazine guarantees an immediate increase in circulation.

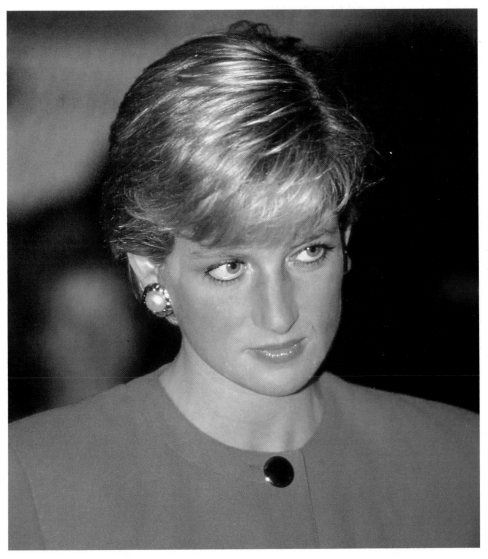

Diana is unquestionably lovely and, as photographers say, looks good on camera. Her hair is naturally glossy, her bones are fine and her complexion flawless — but are her remarkable eyes truly blue?

95

DIANA AND THE MEDIA

The fact is that the media had been waiting for Diana. They had had no substantial figure to focus on for a long time, and Diana incarnated all they needed – youth, beauty, wealth, ancestry, fame, and glamour. The hordes of reporters and photographers who dogged her from the time she took her first uncertain steps on to the world stage were satisfying a deep and ancient need. They knew that for most of their readers the important thing was not the lead story – war, famine, flood, earthquake or political upheaval – but the arrival of Princess Di at a ball dressed in a breathtaking evening gown.

Diana, in fact, is a human icon – a myth that is incomparably more powerful than the truth. She is, literally, the stuff that dreams are made of. However, unlike the transient dream creatures of the pop and movie worlds, the image of Diana will not fade from people's memories; quite the reverse. It has already been calculated that she has been photographed more times than any other human being, and she is still a young woman with at least half her lifetime ahead of her. Her fame is not temporary; nor will her romance with the media prove to be a passing fancy. Even when her youthful beauty changes, first into the sterner lines of middle age, and then into the wrinkles of old age, she will remain a very important lady in the life of her people. A quick glance at the place the Queen Mother holds in the heart of the nation is clear enough indication of that.

But Diana still has a long way to go. For many years she will retain the ability to surprise the world with some new and unexpected trick of elegance or some venture into the uncharted waters of fashion. She will continue to set trends and tens of millions of women will still want to imitate her. Her dresses, suits, hats, shoes, and handbags will still be objects of intense scrutiny by the fashion editors of a thousand newspapers and magazines, and her tastes still influence the way the fashion world moves. Young designers will continue to court her favour, and established designers try to please her because they all know that her approval is the seal of success that no one else can imitate.

The media has two love affairs with Diana. The first is at the 'sharp' end, where photographers fight their continual battles to get their lenses into key

positions for the best shots. The second and complementary love affair is with the editors who commission or pay for the photographs. These, in turn, reflect the profound public interest in this remarkable young woman who rocketed from almost total obscurity to world fame in the space of a few days.

This instant celebrity would have been difficult to take for a mature and sophisticated woman of the world. For a shy girl in her late teens it must have been a shattering experience. But in a sense Diana's inexperience was her own best protection. It did not, of course, take her long to begin to understand what was happening to her and to come to terms with it. A natural strength of character enabled her to retain her coolness and good humour under the most testing circumstances. She became battle hardened without becoming battle scarred. She learned to live with it because it became an integral part of the whole of her adult life. In this she contrasts strongly with, for instance, her father-in-law, the Duke of Edinburgh, who had been an active naval officer before he married Princess Elizabeth in 1947. Used to command and to having people jump about at his orders, he found – and continues to find – it difficult to come to terms with the impertinences and bad manners of some photographers.

Diana, on the other hand, remains ever serene and calm. Her smile never fades, her pace never hastens. She behaves as though the press were not there. This suits them exactly because it means that they can assume she will be entirely predictable. There will never be any unpleasant surprises, such as the occasion when the Duke of Edinburgh allowed a sprinkler system to be turned on and soak them.

This is why there are so few bad pictures of her: those that do exist are usually on the rare occasion when her exquisite fashion sense deserts her (and this usually results from over-anticipating a trend). There are virtually no pictures of Diana frowning, yawning, or doing something silly with her hands. Malicious photographers who specialize in pictures of actresses and film stars caught out in embarrassing situations would be wasting their time with Diana.

There is one exception to this rule. This is the papparazzi, the storm troopers of the photographic world. These pests specialize not so much in embarrassing photographs as in intimate ones. Their pictures, as far as editors are concerned, are on the borderline between the daringly but outrageously revealing and the simply unacceptable. They normally operate from a hidden position and are experts with very long-range lenses. They are prepared to wait days and even weeks to get one photograph they want. One of them snapped the very pregnant Diana in a bikini, and the picture was widely circulated. It was not at all improper but was deeply upsetting to the young Princess.

As the only time the papparazzi could possibly catch Diana would be on holiday, she now runs no risk. At all public occasions they would simply disappear in the jostling throng. And the electronically protected wall at Highgrove is designed to exclude intruders with much more sinister motives than photographers.

Finally, there are occasional official, posed photographs for which Diana is prepared like a work of art. Ironically, she does not show particularly well in these, as her special sparkle and animation are subdued, if not destroyed. The sheer quality of her skin, her hair, and her eyes works against her. She needs movement and life to show her at her best.

But in the wide and frantic world of the working photographer, anxious to get the shot he wants and prepared to go a long way to get it, Diana remains the photographer's favourite model – and the one from whom he can expect most.

Previous page left: Magazine editors, both at home and abroad, know that putting Diana's photograph on the cover is the one sure-fire way of increasing an issue's circulation.

Previous page right: Diana's naturalness and unconcern in the face of hundreds of flash bulbs make her a photographer's dream. Even in the worst possible conditions, she remains unruffled, charming and completely photogenic.

Right: Diana has travelled a long hard road since the days when she ran the gauntlet outside her flat in Coleherne Court. On both public and private occasions, such as the wedding of her friend Anne Bolton, she simply ignores the battalions of cameramen and photographers lying in wait.

CHAPTER 7
QUEEN
DIANA

Diana is now in the full bloom of her womanhood: beautiful, poised, self-assured, conscious of the unique position she holds in society and quietly reconciled to all the demands it makes on her. She is aware of how far she is from the cares, joys, and preoccupations of ordinary mortals and knows that, however close she may have been to her two sons when they were babies, they will never be able to live a conventionally happy family life. She knows that her husband must live a life often separate from hers and that, when he ascends the throne, he will become a different kind of being – a King. However close and intimate their relationship in the early years of their marriage, she will always walk one step behind him.

But this acceptance of her role does not necessarily mean that she would be a 'good' Queen – whatever that may be. It is certainly a role very different from that of a Princess. There still lingers something of a fairytale about the life of a Princess. There is no fairytale about the life of a Queen – and a Queen-Consort at that. How well can 'Shy Princess Di' be considered to have learned all the necessary lessons for the awesome task ahead of her? How will her well-established personality cope with the new set of pressures that will be placed upon her?

Previous page: In a recent British poll, more people recognized Diana than any other member of the Royal Family, with the exception of the Queen Mother.

Left: Diana is almost as well known and as well liked in Continental Europe and the United States as she is in Britain.

ROYAL VIEWPOINTS

To begin to answer these and other questions, we need to consider how the various people involved see Diana now and in her future role. Obviously the key person here is her husband, the Prince of Wales, the future King Charles III.

From as early as he can remember, Charles had been made aware of his destiny and, as a serious-minded boy, youth and adult man, he had taken it all very much to heart. His father has been a particularly hard taskmaster with extremely high expectations of his eldest son, and we know that Charles frequently felt inadequate to the task that lay ahead. Earl Mountbatten, too, who was particularly close to Charles, frequently drew his attention to the shortcomings of the last Prince of Wales, the unfortunate Edward VIII. So Charles was always very conscious of his current and future responsibilities.

Although Diana had been raised as befitted a great lady, she was not brought up as a future queen-consort. No one ever is. There are no training courses in queenship. So when she married Charles when she was a mere girl of 19, she had everything to learn about her future role. Diana was a girl with the tastes and temperament of a normal young woman – she liked pop music and parties, was not keen on science or philosophy, and not used to handling abstract concepts about kingship and royal duty. However seriously she took them, however attentive she was to her patient and anxious husband, however much she loved him, she would never be able to duplicate Charles's 30 years' intensive training course. In any case he was a fully mature man, 12 years older than she was. So it is certain that on occasions Charles was concerned that the earnestness and serious-mindedness built into him were not as strong in his beautiful young wife. He would have had the same doubts about any woman he might have married: no woman ever born could have lived up to expectations as unrealistic as those. But as time went on and Diana performed her public duties with more and more aplomb and expertise, any lingering doubts must have been gradually extinguished until he was completely sure that the woman who was destined to share the throne with him was indeed worthy of this unique honour.

Another key figure in this equation is, of course, the Queen herself. Now one of the most experienced monarchs in the whole of British history, she has mastered the subtle art of reigning without ruling and fully understands the place that the monarch must hold in modern Britain if the monarchy is to survive in an increasingly egalitarian world. She has, therefore, a deep interest in her son's ability to keep the royal ship afloat.

She knew that her son had a highly-developed sense of duty, but obviously he needed a wife, and we know that she was becoming increasingly concerned as Charles progressed through his late twenties and into his early thirties. At first sight Diana seemed a perfect choice. But what were Diana's disadvantages? Did she have any faults that might disqualify her from the high task she would have to perform? She was young, she was irresponsible, maybe she liked dressing up too much. But on consideration, none of these objections could carry much weight. Time would take care of her youth. All normal girls of her age were irresponsible unless they were dreary – and Diana certainly was not dreary. And as for her dressing up, it would appear to work very much to the advantage of royalty. Also Diana was patently and obviously very much in love with Charles.

The other members of the Royal Family would also have a close personal interest in Diana's progress. However close and friendly she may be as Princess

As an ambassadress for Britain, Diana cannot be faulted. Wherever she goes, she gives the impression of being endlessly interested and never pressured for time. Her English rose looks, her tremendous elegance, and her natural charm endear her to all who have the pleasure of meeting her.

of Wales, one day she will be Queen, and the relationship will have to change profoundly. They must have watched her public activities with keen and knowledgeable eyes; any shortcomings would be quickly apparent to them. But she has obviously passed the test. She has shaken the hands of hundreds of mayors, planted a small forest of trees and listened to a thousand speeches with

interest and intelligence. She has sat alertly through dozens of concerts and recitals, eaten her fill of civic lunches without flinching. She has made small talk with politicians and cooed at nurseries of babies. She has read what the papers say about her, and it has neither turned her head nor sickened her. As far as her close royal relations are concerned, her on-the-job training has succeeded.

When people wait hours in the rain to see her, Diana has no intention of disappointing them.

THE BRITISH PEOPLE

As far as the British people are concerned Diana is very firmly established in their minds and hearts. The latest *Mori* poll shows, for instance, that she is even better known than the Queen. (99 per cent of interviewees recognized her picture, 98 per cent the Queen. The Queen Mother scored 100 per cent.) People felt they 'knew' her as well if not better than the Queen herself. A very high proportion considered Diana the most attractive member of the Royal Family; more than twice as many as favoured the runner-up, the Duchess of York. Diana comes top in the table of the pleasantest personality in the Royal Family, the most modern, and the woman most women would like to be. She is unquestionably firmly embedded in the affections of the British people.

Left: Diana took time to help a young flower-giver in Nottingham present his bouquet.

Right: After the birth of Wills, Diana was inundated with gifts for her young son. She was clearly delighted with this very cuddly bear given to her in Canterbury.

108

Diana has succeeded beyond all expectation in establishing a specific role as Princess of Wales and in finding a special place in the hearts of the nation. She seems firmly set on course to be just as successful as a future Queen.

A QUEEN IN WAITING

As future Queen-Consort Diana certainly passes muster. She has learned how to cope with people and public occasions on her own and she also knows when she must act as a foil for her husband and let Charles lead. She is an innately pleasant and sociable young woman. Like the Queen Mother, she genuinely likes people and, where her interest is seriously engaged, she can be a very effective champion for any cause she adopts. At the same time, she is mature enough to know that it is unwise to become involved in too many worthy causes. Nevertheless she will be a kind and caring Queen.

When will it all happen? Nobody knows, of course. Happily, the Queen is in excellent health; if she lives as long as her mother, she could still be Queen in 2015, by which time Charles would be 67 and Diana a ripe 54. All in all, the prospect of Charles ascending the throne before he is 50 appears remote. So there is almost certain to be a substantial waiting time for both the Prince and Princess of Wales.

It has been suggested that the Queen might abdicate. There are plenty of Continental precedents and the Queen has served Britain well for nearly 40 years. Many loyal and loving subjects would approve if she decided to retire to the country with her dogs and horses to lead the life of a country lady that we know she enjoys. However, there is no British tradition of abdication.

There is one new lesson that Diana will have to learn: how to assist her husband in the transition from reigning over the last vestiges of a once vast Empire into the first monarch in a largely republican Europe. Not King *of* Europe, but King *in* Europe. Here, paradoxically, Diana really comes into her own. While Prince Charles is little known in continental Europe, Diana is as much a megastar there as she is in Britain. Her photograph on the cover of French, German, and Italian magazines – to name but three states of the EEC – are as common as they are on the bookstalls of Britain.

Ironically, Diana is one of the biggest 'invisibles' the country has, unquantifiable but hugely influential in promoting Britain and British exports. She already commands a unique position in Europe, so she has a function above and alongside her domestic role as Princess of Wales: she is also, in all but name, Princess of Europe. As Britain is more and more closely integrated with Europe, this could be a major factor in her role as Queen of Great Britain.

No one knows when Diana and Charles will be called to take up the responsibilities of monarchy, nor, indeed, when the cloak of kingship will fall on young William's shoulders. Meanwhile, Queen Consort in waiting – and Queen Mother in waiting – Diana continues to develop and mature, building on her many strengths and acquiring new experience.